PRISON

TO

PRAISE

AND

POWER

IN

PRAISE

PRISON TO PRAISE

Because it has had such dramatic impact upon its readers, this book has been translated, printed and distributed in more languages than any other contemporary Christian book. Printed in the following languages, it continues to be a best-seller.

Afrikaans
Arabic
Chinese
Czechoslovakian
Danish
Dutch
English
Filipino
Finnish
French
German

Greek
Greenlandic
Hindi
Hungarian
Indonesian
Italian
Japanese
Korean
Marathi
Norwegian

Pidgin
Portuguese
Romanian
Spanish
Swahili
Swedish
Tamil
Thai
Tranomaizina
Twi
Urdu

Prison to Praise is also printed and distributed in:

Australia
Austria
Brazil
Canada
England

Ireland
Mexico
New Zealand
Nova Scotia
Switzerland

PRISON TO PRAISE

Contents

Chapters

1

Prisoner

There was the touch of cold metal against my left wrist and the harsh voice in my ear: "This is the FBI. You are under arrest."

I'd been relaxing in the back seat of the car with my left arm hanging out the window. The car was stolen and I was AWOL from the Army.

Being AWOL didn't bother me. It was the getting caught that hurt my pride. I'd always considered myself capable of doing my own thing and getting away with it. Now I had to suffer the humiliation of the jail cell, stand in line for lousy cold chow, go back to the lonely cell and the hard bunk with nothing to do but stare at the wall. How could I have been stupid enough to get into a mess like this?

I'd been a pretty independent fellow from the time I was twelve. That's when my father died suddenly, leaving my mother alone with three boys to raise. My brothers were seven and one, and Mother started taking in washings and went on relief to keep us alive. She always talked about Dad being in heaven and how God would take care of us, but with the intensity of a twelve-year-old I turned in fury against a God who could treat us that way.

I delivered papers after school until long after dark each night, determined to make my way in life. I was going to make the most of it. Somehow I felt I had it coming. I had a right to grab for all I could get.

When Mother remarried, I went to live with some of Dad's old friends. I went to high school, but never quit working. After school and all summer I worked. As a food packer, shipping clerk, linotype operator, and one summer as a lumberjack in Pennsylvania.

I started college, but ran out of money and had to go to work. This time I got a job with B&W Steel as a steel chipper and grinder. Not a very pleasant job, but it kept me in top physical condition. Part of staying ahead in the rat race of the world was being in top shape physically, and I didn't intend to lose out on any count.

I never did want to join the Army. I wanted to go off to sea with the Merchant Marine. I couldn't think of a more glamorous way to get into action in World War II.

To join the Merchant Marine I had to get re-classified 1-A with the draft board that had given me a deferment to go to college. Before I could make it back to the Merchant Marine, the Army inducted me. They told me I could volunteer for the Navy, which I did, but a freak incident kept me out. I failed the eye test simply because I'd been reading the wrong line on the chart by mistake! So there, against all my efforts, I landed in basic training at Ft. McClellan, Alabama.

I was bored to death. The training was a breeze, and looking for excitement, I volunteered for airborne training at Fort Benning, Georgia.

A rebel at heart, my biggest problem always was in getting along with my superiors. Somehow they picked on me in spite of all my efforts to remain in the background. Once, during physical training in a sawdust pit, I spat on the ground without thinking. The Sergeant saw me, and descended like a storm cloud. "Pick that up in your mouth and carry it out of the area!" he screamed.

You've got to be kidding, I thought, but his red, glowering face indicated he was not. So, humiliated and seething with resentment carefully hidden, I picked up the spit - and a mouthful of sawdust - and carried it "out of the area."

The compensation came when we got our first chance to jump from an airplane in flight. This was living! The kind of excitement I was hungering for. Over the roar of the plane engines came the shouted command: "Get ready. . .stand up. . .hook up. . .stand in the door. . .GO!"

The blast of air makes you feel like a leaf in a gale - and then, as the rope attached to your parachute reaches its end, a bone-jarring jolt. You feel like you've been hit by a ten-ton truck.

Then, as your brain clears, you're in a beautiful silent world; billowing above is the parachute - a giant white arc of silk.

I was a paratrooper, and earned the honor of wearing the glistening jump boots.

Still, I wanted more excitement and volunteered for advanced training as a Demolition Expert. I wanted in on the war effort, and the hotter the action the better, I thought.

After demolition school I returned to Fort Benning to wait for orders to go overseas. I pulled guard at the stockade, had KP, and waited some more. Patience was not my strong point. At the rate the Army was moving, I figured I might miss out on the fun altogether, scrubbing pots and pans till the war ended.

I wasn't going to sit around doing nothing, and with a friend, I decided to go over the hill.

We simply walked out of the camp one day, stole a car, and headed for anyplace. Just in case someone was looking for us, we dropped the first car and stole another and finally ended up in Pittsburgh, Pennsylvania. There we ran out of spending money and decided to pull a stickup.

I had the gun and my friend waited in the car. We'd picked a store that looked like an easy job. My plan was to pull the telephone wiring so they couldn't call the police. Inside the store, I yanked on the telephone wire as hard as I could, but it wouldn't budge. I was frustrated. The gun was in my pocket, the cash register was full of money, but the line to the police was still there. I wasn't about to invite disaster.

So I went back to the car to tell my buddy, and we were just sitting there in the back seat, eating green apples and talking, when the long arm of the law finally caught up with us. We didn't know it, but a six-state alarm had gone out for us, and the FBI was hot on our heels.

Our search for adventure had ended in a pretty sad flop. I was back in the stockade at Fort Benning where I'd been a guard only a few months earlier. I was sentenced to six months' confinement and immediately started a campaign to get overseas. My fellow prisoners laughed and said, "You wouldn't have gone AWOL if you wanted to go overseas."

I kept insisting I'd gone AWOL because I got bored waiting to be sent overseas.

4

At last my pleas were heard. I was placed on overseas shipment and went "under guard" to Camp Kilmer, N.J., where I was placed in the stockade to wait for our ship to Europe.

At last, I was on my way. Almost, anyway. The night before our ship was due to sail I was called to the Commander's office where I learned that I wouldn't be sailing with the rest of the men.

"The FBI wants you held and returned to Pittsburgh, Pennsylvania."

Once more I felt the cold steel of handcuffs, and under armed guard I returned to Pittsburgh where a stern judge read the charges and asked: "Guilty or not guilty; how do you plead?"

My mother was there and her tear-filled eyes made me cringe. Not that I was sorry for what I'd done. I wanted out of there and on with some fast living, the sooner the better.

"Guilty, Sir." I had been caught red-handed and somehow I determined it would be the last time. I would learn the tricks and play it safe from now on.

The district attorney carefully explained my past life to the judge who asked the investigating officers for their recommendation.

"Your honor, we recommend leniency."

"What do you want, soldier?" the judge asked me.

"I want to go back in the Army and get into the war," was all I could say.

"I sentence you to five years in the Federal Penitentiary."

His words hit me like a load of bricks from the skies. I was nineteen and would be twenty-four when I got out. I saw my whole life go down the drain.

"Your sentence is temporarily suspended and you will be returned to the Army."

Saved, thank heaven! In less than an hour I was released. But first the district attorney gave me a stern lecture and explained that if I left the Army in less than five years I should report back to his office.

Free at last! I headed back to Fort Dix, New Jersey, only to get another load of bricks on my head. At Fort Dix they looked at my papers and sent me back to the stockade to serve out my six months' sentence for AWOL!

At this point I had only one thought in my head. I wanted to get into the war or bust. Again I started my campaign to get on an overseas shipment. I pestered the command until finally, when four months of my time was completed, I was released. Soon I was on my way across the Atlantic aboard the *Mauretania*.

We were piled six high in the hold, and I was lucky enough to get the top berth. That way I missed the shower of vomit those on the lower berths often received.

Not that I really would have cared. I was thrilled to be on my way, and didn't waste any time. I was out to get as much excitement and as much profit as possible out of the war effort. I had developed one talent during my confinement that now came in handy. I had become quite adept at gambling, and the days and nights of our crossing were spent in this worthwhile endeavor. I accumulated a nice little pile of money, and the only thing that reminded me of the circumstances of our voyage was a brief encounter with a German sub that tried to hit us and missed.

In England we were put on trains that took us to the English Channel. There we boarded small boats and moved out into the choppy waters of the channel. It rained cats and dogs, and on the French side we had to jump into waist-high water and wade ashore.

On the beach we stood dripping wet in line waiting for cold C-rations. Then we rushed again for a train headed east. Without stopping, we crossed France and were transferred to trucks taking us into Belgium. We got there just in time for the Battle of the Bulge with the 82nd Airborne Division.

On my first day in combat, the Commanding Officer saw my record as a Demolition Expert and put me to work making small bombs out of a pile of plastic explosives. The pile was about three feet high, and I pulled up a log and went to work. Another soldier joined me, and I learned that he had been with the unit for many months. While he was telling me about his experiences with the 82nd Airborne, I looked across a field at incoming artillery exploding. The explosions came closer and closer to our position. Out of the corner of my eye I kept watching the other soldier, wondering when he'd give the signal to dive for cover. He had all the experience, and I was just a green replacement; I wasn't going to chicken out.

The explosions came nearer, and my fear mounted. If one of those rounds landed near us . . .the pile of bombs would make one giant crater.

The other fellow sat there paying no attention to the artillery. I wanted desperately to dive for cover, but I wasn't about to show myself a coward. At last the explosions were on the other side of us. They had missed!

Two days later I discovered why the other soldier had played it so cool. The two of us were walking through a forest known to be heavily mined. I carefully examined the trail for any signs of booby traps, but the other fellow was paying no attention to where he was walking. I finally said: "Why aren't you watching for mines?"

7

"I hope I step on one," he said. "I'm sick and tired of this rotten mess. I want to die."

From that day I kept as much distance as possible between the two of us!

Combat with the 82nd Airborne provided ample excitement. But some of the ugly experiences made further harsh impressions in my angry mind.

At the close of the war I went with the 508th Airborne Regiment to Frankfurt, Germany, where I was selected to serve as guard for General of the Army, Dwight D. Eisenhower. This was a proud moment in my life. I, Merlin Carothers, a personal guard for a Five-star General! I felt I had finally become "big man on campus."

I would have liked to see more action, but the spoils of war weren't so bad either. We lived in plush apartment buildings that had belonged to top German officials. The previous occupants must have had no more than five minutes' notice before they departed. We found family picture albums, weapons and even jewels. My off-duty time was spent in searching for "treasure."

My on-duty time was always fun. One evening I was assigned duty at a gate leading into General Eisenhower's Headquarters Compound. Something special was up. The Duty Officer said, "Pfc. Carothers, this could be a big night. I'll fill you in later."

Some time later the Duty Officer came back and said, "Here it is, Carothers. The W.A.C. Commanding Officer is having a dance for her girls next week, but she didn't invite the paratroopers. When our C.O. called and asked her why, she said she didn't want any "overpaid killers" at their dance.

"The rules say that all assigned female personnel must be inside this gate not later than 9:00 p.m. After

9:00 p.m. no W.A.C. (Women's Army Corps) will pass through this gate until I personally escort them. Take no flak from anyone. I've put you here because I know you won't!"

A few minutes after 9:00 p.m. a jeep, driven by an Army Sergeant, pulled up to the gate. A W.A.C. enlisted girl was seated beside the soldier. I said, "The W.A.C. must get out and stand here by the gate."

"She what?" The Sergeant's anger exploded!

"You heard me."

"Why?"

"No reason. Miss, get out of the jeep now and stand beside me."

Never had I spoken to a Sergeant this way. If he had been an airborne trooper I probably wouldn't have dared.

The Sergeant unloaded a few dozen curse words, but then turned around and left. He knew that as a guard assigned to a gate I had total authority.

From 9:00 until 9:45, twenty W.A.C.s arrived. On previous nights they had come in whenever they desired, but tonight was different. I was in the middle of the hurricane. They were mad - very mad. Such language I heard!

At 10:45 a staff car, driven by a Colonel, pulled up. Never in my career had I even spoken to a full Colonel. I politely gave him my message. "The W.A.C. officer that is with you must join these other ladies who are standing by me."

"Out of the way, Soldier! She is not going to leave this vehicle."

"Yes, Sir, she must."

"Soldier, I give you a Direct Order. Move out of the way. We are going through."

A Direct Order is the strongest language an officer can use on a soldier. But he was trying to bluff the wrong private.

In true cowboy fashion I slapped the "45 automatic" from my holster, pulled back the hammer and said, "Miss, step down and join the others. Colonel, turn this vehicle around *now* and leave!"

He did.

At 11:00 p.m. the Duty Officer arrived in a jeep. He told the W.A.C. with the lowest rank to get into his jeep and then said, "Ladies, I'll be back to pick all of you up - one at a time."

The next day the W.A.C. Commander called our C.O. and invited all the airborne troopers to attend her dance.

I was still looking for excitement, and once I almost got more than I bargained for. We were loaded on airplanes for a parachute jump. It was to be a routine training exercise, but we were told that Marlene Dietrich, the movie actress, would be on the ground watching the jump. We were all hoping to land near her.

As soon as I left the plane I began to scan the ground below to see if I could locate the "lady with the beautiful legs." Suddenly I was aware that something was horribly wrong. Around me in the air were terrible screams, and the roar of an airplane engine seemed suddenly to burst right on top of me.

Several hundred troopers were in the air and an airplane had lost engine power and was diving right through us! Parachutes were cut off, and men were plunging to the ground. They were falling all around the spot where Miss Dietrich was standing. My parachute was intact, and when I reached the ground there were dead men all around, and the plane was exploding in flames.

In Frankfurt I had plenty of free time. My idea of a good time usually involved a considerable amount of drinking. It happened that I drank myself into a state of oblivion and other soldiers told me what pranks I had pulled in town the night before. Once I had stretched myself flat on the floor of a German streetcar and dared anyone to walk over me. The other soldiers had roared with laughter and found the whole incident uproariously funny. It never occurred to me that my behavior probably didn't help the image of the American Occupation Army.

I discovered that black marketeering was a quicker and more reliable source of income than gambling. I bought cigarettes from other soldiers for ten dollars a carton. With a suitcase full, I went to the black-market area in town where I could sell the cartons for one hundred dollars apiece. The black-market area was a frequent site of robberies, beatings, and murder, but I didn't care. I kept one hand on a loaded, cocked "45" in my pocket.

Soon I had a suitcase full of ten dollar bills in military money known as scrip. The only problem was to find a way to get the money back to the United States. Tight control limited each soldier to sending home only the amount he was paid by the Army. I stayed awake nights trying to figure a way to beat the system.

At the post office I watched the men line up to convert their monthly pay into money orders. Each man had to have his finance card which listed the exact amount he had been paid. I observed one man with a pile of finance cards, a bag of money, and an armed guard. He was company clerk and was getting money orders for his entire company. I suddenly realized that all I needed was a pile of finance cards!

I located the unit finance clerk and soon learned that he would be willing to provide me with the finance cards for five dollars apiece. I was in business.

I set myself up as the company clerk of my own private company. With the money and the finance cards I went to the post office and had the money orders made out without a hitch!

With this setup I now found new ways to accumulate the military scrip money. I learned that men coming from Berlin would give $1,000 in scrip for a $100 money order. I gladly obliged and then converted the $900 into my own money order. I was on my way to becoming very rich!

The Army announced the decision to send some men to universities throughout Europe. I took the examinations, was selected, and sent to Bristol University in England. The courses I took were far less important than the fact that we were surrounded by girls who spoke English.

But I did make some steps toward what I believed was my future. I took a course in English Law and another in Business Law. I wanted to know how "the system" worked so I could beat it.

When the university course ended I was transferred back to Germany. There awaited exciting news. My time to return to the U.S. had arrived! I packed my suitcase full of $100 money orders and headed for the glorious shores of home.

At Fort Dix, N.J., they tried to get all of us to sign up for the Army Reserves. The Sergeant giving the pitch said, "Everyone who wants to sign up for the

Reserves step up here, sign, and I'll give you your discharge. If you don't sign up now you will have to stay and hear a one-hour lecture on why you *should* sign up."

One hour longer in the Army? No way, I thought. I stepped forward and signed their paper. That split-second decision affected the rest of my life.

I received the long-coveted paper stating I was now a civilian. Free! I had no desire to ever see the inside of an Army post again. I had plenty of money, and life ahead looked rosy.

There was a problem of converting my suitcase full of money orders into crisp, green bills. I couldn't very well walk into the post office in my hometown, Ellwood City, Pennsylvania, and dump the whole stack on the counter. Finally I thought of a solution. One by one I began to send the money orders to a post office in New York. Soon the money began filtering back.

My experiences with the law so far had taught me that I had better get into a profession where I would be able to operate safely within every available loophole. I had always wanted to become a lawyer, so I began the necessary steps to enroll in law school in Pittsburgh, Pennsylvania.

2

Set Free

Grandmother was a sweet old lady, and I thought a great deal of Grandfather, but going to visit them was still an ordeal I avoided whenever possible. They made me nervous. Grandmother always found an opportunity to talk about God.

"I'm doing fine," I'd say. "Don't worry about me."

But she would insist: "You need to give your life to Christ, Merlin."

It bugged me more than I wanted to admit. I hated to hurt Grandmother's feelings, but I didn't have time for any of that religious stuff. I'd just begun to live!

One Sunday evening shortly after I'd come back from Germany, I went to see Grandmother and Grandfather. I quickly realized I'd made a mistake. They were getting ready to go to church.

"Come go with us, Merlin," Grandmother said. "We haven't seen you for so long; we'd love to have you come."

I squirmed in my chair. How could I tactfully get out of this one?

"I'd like to," I said finally. "But some friends have already asked if they could come pick me up."

Grandmother looked disappointed, and as soon as I could get to the phone I began calling everyone I knew. To my dismay I couldn't find anyone who was free to come pick me up.

It was getting close to church time, and I couldn't say to my grandparents: "I just don't want to go."

At the zero hour I had no choice. Off we went together.

The church service was held in a barn, but everyone there seemed to be happy. *Poor people*, I thought, *they don't know anything about real life out there in the world, or they wouldn't waste an evening in a barn.*

The singing began and I picked up a hymn book to follow the words. At least I had to look as if I was with it.

Suddenly I heard a deep voice speak directly in my ear.

"What-what did you say?" I whirled around to find no one behind me.

There was the voice again: "Tonight you must make a decision for Me. If you don't, it will be too late."

I shook my head and said automatically: "Why?"

"It just will be!"

Was I losing my marbles? But the voice was real. It was God, and He knew me! In a flash I suddenly saw it. Why hadn't I seen it before? God was real; He was the answer. In Him was everything I had ever searched for.

"Yes, God," I heard myself mutter. "I'll do it; whatever You want."

The service went on, but I was in another world. This was crazy, but I knew God!

Grandfather was deep in thought beside me. I didn't know it then, but he told me about it later. He was carrying on his own battle with God. For years he'd been smoking and chewing tobacco. Forty years of addiction to the weed had him hooked. Many a time he'd tried to quit, but had been seized with violent headaches and soon was back to chewing and smoking heavier than before.

Now he was sitting next to me in the meeting making his own commitment. "God, if you'll change Merlin, I'll give up my chewing and smoking even if it kills me."

No wonder Grandfather nearly collapsed when I went forward at the end of the meeting to make public the decision I'd made during the singing!

Years later I was at his bedside when his time came to die. He looked up at me and smiled. "Merlin," he said, "I kept my promise to God."

That Sunday night I couldn't wait to get home and read the Bible. I wanted to know God, and I read hungrily page after page. I had a wonderful feeling of excitement inside. It was even better than jumping off an airplane with a parachute. That night God had reached down inside me, and I was changed into a new being. I felt as if I was standing on the threshold of exciting adventures the likes of which I couldn't even begin to imagine. The God of Abraham, Isaac, and Jacob was still alive; the God who parted the Red Sea and spoke through a burning bush and sent His Son to die on a cross - He was my Father too!

I could suddenly understand what my earthly father had tried to tell me. When he was thirty-six years old he was confined to a bed for the first time in his life. Three days later his heart stopped. The doctor was there with an injection, and my father's heart began beating again. He opened his eyes and said: "That won't be necessary, Doctor. I am going to leave now." He raised himself up in bed and looked around the room with a radiant glow on his face.

17

"Look!" he said. "They are here to take me!" With that he lay back and was gone.

My father had known Jesus Christ as his personal friend and Savior. He had been ready to go.

Now I felt ready too, but even as I voiced the thought to myself, I became aware of an uneasiness, a gnawing at the back of my mind. What was wrong? Show me, God!

Gradually the thought became clearer. The money! All that money. It wasn't mine; I had to give it back!

The decision made, I breathed a sigh of relief. I couldn't wait to get rid of that money. It was like a sickness inside me, and I knew that feeling would be there until the money was gone.

I told the post office, but they said it wasn't any concern of theirs because I hadn't stolen the money orders. I could do with them as I liked.

I still had a whole bunch that I hadn't cashed in yet, so I took the suitcase into the bathroom and began to flush piles of one hundred dollar money orders down the toilet. With each flush I felt a mounting flood of joy inside.

That still left me with the money I had already cashed. I wrote the U.S. Treasury Department and told them how I had acquired the money. They wrote back asking if I had any evidence of how I had gotten the money and the money orders. It was too late; the evidence was flushed down the drain! I told them I had no proof, just the money, and they advised me that all they could do was to accept the money into the Conscience Fund.

Once again I was a poor man, but I would gladly have given away everything I owned for that new life and joy I felt within.

There was one more shadow of the past to be encountered. I returned to Pittsburgh and reported to the district attorney. There were three years remaining on my sentence, and I would now have to be on a parole status for these years. This meant regular reporting and supervision by a parole officer.

The district attorney received me and asked a clerk to get my records. He glanced at them and looked surprised.

"Do you know what you have received?" I knew I'd received Christ, but that could hardly have gotten into my record already.

"No, sir."

"You have received a presidential pardon, signed by President Truman!"

"A pardon?"

"That means your record is completely clear. Just as if you had never gotten involved with the law."

I wanted to shout for joy. "Why did I get it?"

The district attorney smiled. "It has something to do with your excellent combat record."

He explained that I was free to go and do anything I wanted to; my case was closed.

"If you ever apply for a federal job you are completely eligible."

"Thank you, Lord." I was overwhelmed. Not only were my sins washed away and the case closed at Calvary, but God had given me a clean start in the eyes of the United States government as well. Not that I ever thought I'd be looking for a job with them again!

But what was I going to do? My motives for becoming a lawyer had been questionable. It seemed clear that God did not want me in that profession. Soon the thought became very persistent. I was to become a minister! Me, in the pulpit? The thought seemed preposterous. "You know me, Lord," I argued.

"I like excitement, adventure, even danger. I wouldn't make a very good preacher."

It seemed that God had His plans for me all set. I couldn't sleep nights, and the longer I thought and prayed, the more exciting the whole idea became. If God could make a preacher out of an ex-jailbird, paratrooper, gambler, and black-marketeer, that would be a greater adventure into the unknown than anything I'd ever tried before.

I enrolled in Marion College, a church-related school in Marion, Indiana, and I must have been the most excited student on campus.

To supplement my income from the GI bill, I worked six hours a day in a foundry. I wanted to get through school as fast as possible so I got special permission to take twenty-one hours rather than the maximum seventeen hours allowed per semester.

I worked from 2:00 p.m. until 8:00 p.m., studied until 12:00 p.m., slept until 4:00 a.m., and then studied until 8:00 a.m. when it was time to go to school.

One Sunday I got my first chance to preach in the local jail. I held onto the bars and begged the men to give their lives to Christ. Every week prisoners knelt, holding on to the bars from the other side, and wept their way to faith in Christ.

I went back to school floating on a cloud.

Saturday nights were free, and I got a group of students together to hold outdoor services on the courthouse steps in the center of Marion. To our delight, people came forward to accept Christ. After the service we walked up and down the streets, urging anyone who would listen to let Jesus come into their lives.

I had never been so busy, yet I felt as if I couldn't work hard enough for Jesus Christ. He had saved my life; the least I could do was give Him my time.

I finished the four-year course in two-and-a-half years and enrolled at Asbury Seminary in Wilmore, Kentucky. God provided me with a Methodist circuit of four churches where I served as student pastor. Every week I drove the round trip of two hundred miles to serve my churches. For this each of them gave me five dollars a week and I was able to eat bountifully each weekend.

By squeezing everything I could into the schedule, I completed the three-year seminary in two years. At last I had made it to my goal. I was a minister! I had worked so long and so hard that I didn't quite know how to stop. But this was it; this was what God had called me to do. I was sent to the Methodist church in Claypool, Indiana, for my first full-time assignment. I threw myself into the work with all the zeal I could muster, and slowly the three churches in the circuit began to grow. The offerings increased, the attendance grew and my salary went up.

Young people accepted Christ in growing numbers, and my flock accepted and loved me and put up with the blunders of a young minister.

Still I felt a growing restlessness within me. There was a void, an emptiness, almost a boredom. Increasingly, my thoughts were drawn toward the Army chaplaincy. I knew the soldier, his thoughts and his temptations. Did God want me to serve the men in uniform? I prayed about it. "I'll go if You want me to go, Lord; I'll stay if You want me to stay. . . ."

Gradually the pull toward the Army got stronger. In 1953 I volunteered for the chaplaincy and was accepted. It couldn't have happened if I hadn't received that presidential pardon. God had known and blessed me in this special way.

After three months at chaplains' school, I was sent to join the airborne troopers at Fort Campbell, Kentucky.

At the first opportunity, I boarded an airplane and heard the familiar words: "Get ready; stand up; hook up; stand in the door. . .GO."

I felt the thrust of the wind and the shock as the parachute opened. It still felt like a ten-ton truck hitting me. I was back where I belonged!

3

The Search

It's exciting to be a chaplain, and it was excitement I'd been looking for. I went everywhere with the men. In the air, on the ground, climbing mountains, going on marches, undergoing physical conditioning. In the billets, offices, on the field, or in the mess hall - everywhere I had opportunities to tell men what God wanted to do for them.

I enjoyed every minute of the physical hardships. On jungle-expert training in Panama we all lived in and lived off the fruits of the jungle. The steaming jungle rapidly took its toll, and some men had to be carried out on stretchers. I learned how comfortable it can be to lie in a puddle of mud!

At Fort Campbell I had the opportunity to become a pilot, something I'd always wanted. With a friend I bought an old airplane held together mainly by chewing gum and rubber bands, it seemed. The plane had no radio equipment and we had to fly by sight or instinct. Once I got completely lost and suddenly found myself escorted by two Army planes. They motioned for me to land, and I found I'd been flying over Fort

23

Knox, Kentucky. The angry security police informed me I was lucky not to have been shot down.

Our flying came to an abrupt end when my partner crashlanded the plane in a cornfield.

While stationed at Fort Bragg, North Carolina, I went with the 82nd Airborne Division to the Dominican Republic. This was a small police action, but thirty-nine paratroopers were lost.

Back at Fort Bragg, I continued parachuting and finally received the coveted Army award of Master Parachutist.

From outward appearances all was well. My life was full and exciting and I was doing God's work. Maybe that was part of the problem. I was doing God's work. I didn't like to admit it, but I often became too tense when I talked to the men about God's love for them. Converting them was my business and I struggled hard.

I was always aware that I was falling woefully short of the perfection I longed for. Somehow it was always just beyond the horizon.

As a young boy I'd heard my mother and grandmother talk about the need for purity and holiness in living. They were Wesleyan and Free Methodist and spoke of the work of the Holy Spirit in the life of the Christian.

Whatever it was, I certainly lacked it. I read books about the deeper life of prayer, and went to camp meetings to hear others preach about the power of God.

I didn't see much of that power in my own life, and I desperately longed for it. I wanted to be used of God, and everywhere I looked were people in need. I just didn't have what it took to meet their needs.

A friend gave me a book about an eastern cult claiming to know the method of opening people's minds to the power of God. I learned to lie on a board with my feet elevated and to practice silent meditation.

I began to read everything I could find about psychic phenomena, hypnotism, and spiritism, hoping to find a clue to the secret of letting God's Spirit work in and through me.

About this time I went to Korea and there, in an accident, my glasses shattered into my right eye. Sixty percent of the vision in that eye was gone. The cornea was scarred, and the doctors said vision would never return.

Now, where was the power of God? Christ had walked the earth and healed the blind. He said that greater things even than He had done, those who followed after Him would do.

I went to Seoul twice for eye operations. The verdict was negative. I prayed. Everything in me rebelled against accepting a God of salvation, a God who is omnipotent creator, a God whose name I preach to men who face death on the battlefield, as a God without the power to heal. But where was the key? How was that power released through men? I had to know.

On my third flight to Seoul for a visit to the surgeon, I was sitting in the airplane when suddenly there was a strong sensation within me. It wasn't an audible voice, but something definitely communicated, saying: "Your eyes are going to be all right."

I knew God had spoken. He had spoken to me, just as clearly as He did that Sunday evening in the barn back in Pennsylvania.

The surgeon in Seoul shook his head and said: "Sorry, Chaplain, there's nothing we can do for your eye." Instead of feeling discouragement, I was elated. God had spoken; I trusted Him.

A few months later I had a sudden urge to go back to the doctor to check on my eye. After the examination he looked astonished. "I don't understand," he said. "Your eye is perfectly well."

God had done it! I was thrilled and more determined than ever to research every avenue of contact with His power.

I returned to the United States in 1963, went back to Chaplains' School for six months and was assigned to Fort Bragg, N.C., in 1964.

Here I continued studying hypnosis with renewed vigor, and got involved in the Spiritual Frontiers movement led by Arthur Ford. I had heard that many ministers were drawn to this movement. In Arthur Ford's home I saw firsthand evidence of the workings of a spirit world completely separate from our known rational world. I was fascinated.

But was it scriptural? There were pangs of nagging doubts in the back of my mind. The spirits were unquestionably real, but the Bible speaks of spirits other than God's Holy Spirit, and talks about spiritual wickedness in high places (Ephesians 6). The Bible calls these spirits our enemies, Satan's own forces, and warns us to test all spirits to be sure we aren't being manipulated by the enemy. Satan can cleverly counterfeit the work of the Holy Spirit.

I felt reasonably sure that I wasn't getting myself into a blind alley. These spirits, and the people I met in the movement, did, after all, speak very highly of Christ. They certainly recognized Him as the Son of God and a great spiritual leader who worked many miracles.

The goal for us, they taught, is to become like Christ in all things, since we are also sons of God.

I traveled many miles to talk with people who knew something about the subject, studied books on hypnotism, spoke to doctors, even wrote the Library of Congress. For here, I felt, was the avenue I, as mortal man, could use to help others.

I didn't know I was on dangerous ground. Subtly, but surely, I had begun to look at Jesus Christ as someone much like myself. Someone I could be like if I tried hard enough.

I had greatly underestimated the powers of the enemy. I didn't know it then, but hypnosis is potentially very dangerous spiritually, leaving the subject wide-open for impulses from the realm of Satan.

Oh yes, I was also falling into the trap of thinking of Satan as a bad character with horns from a realm of imagery. He certainly couldn't pose a threat to the sophisticated man of the twentieth century.

C.S. Lewis once said that Satan's cleverest trick is to convince the world that he doesn't exist.

My faith had become damaged and seriously undermined, although I didn't know it yet. The change was so subtle. Perhaps the fine line was crossed when I found myself talking about Jesus as teacher and miracle worker and failing to mention that He died on a cross for us, that His blood cleanses us from sin.

Satan quoted Scriptures even in Jesus' time. He still does, and really doesn't mind when we do. But he would like to see us forget about the cross, the blood, and the resurrected Jesus.

Paul speaks about the secret of the Christian life in Colossians 1:27. The secret is Christ in us. Not that we become like Him, but that He lives in us and transforms us from within. Others may look at us and say we appear to be Christlike, but not because we have become more worthy or holy or spiritual or pure. He lives in us. That's the secret.

The subtle danger of the so-called, "Christian Spiritualist Movement" or "Spiritual Frontiers Movement" is that it would lead men to try to copy Christ and appropriate spiritual powers for themselves, and so commit the original sin of Satan, the fallen angel, who wanted to be like God Himself.

Without Christ as Savior, without the cross, there would be no plan of salvation, no possible way to be forgiven of sin. In fact, there would be no gospel.

I was falling into the trap. My motives were pure; I honestly wanted power to help others overcome their problems and their sicknesses of body and mind.

It took an act of God to open my eyes to the error of my ways.

4

Be Filled

For some time I had been going to a small weekly prayer group near Fort Bragg. One evening, Ruth, a member of the group, was visibly moved during a prayer session. I had watched her during several meetings and often thought I would like to ask her how she had come to experience such obvious joy in her life. Unlike some of the rest of us, she seemed to be filled continuously with a joy I certainly had felt only on rare occasions in my life.

This particular evening Ruth confided in me: "I was so blessed I almost prayed out loud in tongues!"

"You almost what?" I was horrified.

"Prayed in tongues," Ruth said brightly.

I lowered my voice and looked around to see if we were being watched. "Ruth, you could have ruined our group! Whatever has come over you?"

Ruth laughed heartily. "I've been praying in tongues ever since I received the Baptism in the Holy Spirit."

"What is that?" I'd never heard the term before.

Ruth patiently explained that it was the same experience that the disciples had at Pentecost. "I experienced my own Pentecost." She smiled with unmistakable radiance.

"I thought you were Baptist." I felt shaken.

"I am, but God is moving in all denominations."

I had heard rumors of a wave of emotionalism invading the churches, people getting off on fads and losing faith in Christ. I had heard some tales about Pentecostals being "drunk in the spirit," whatever that meant, and having wild orgies. I knew Ruth needed help badly.

I put my hand on her arm. "Be careful, Ruth," I said earnestly. "You're playing with dangerous stuff. I'll be praying for you, and if you need help, call me."

Ruth smiled and patted my hand. "Thank you, Merlin. I appreciate your concern."

Some time later she called me.

"Merlin, a group called Camp Farthest Out is having a retreat at Morehead City. We'd like you to go." It sounded like something I'd better stay away from. I tactfully replied that I would go if I could, which meant that I wouldn't be able to.

Within the next week several others called. A businessman reminded me that I would need my golf clubs. A lady from Raleigh telephoned to tell me that she had arranged for all my expenses to be paid if I would go. Someone else called to say I could bring another minister free of charge. This was too much. How could I resist all this genuine interest in my spiritual well-being? I said, "Thank you, I'll go."

I got in touch with a Presbyterian minister friend and invited him to come along. He hedged.

"It's an all-expenses-paid trip at a resort hotel!"

"I'll go."

On the way Dick said: "Merlin, why are we going to this thing?"

"I don't know," I said. "But it's for free, so let's enjoy it."

In the hotel lobby we were greeted with such warm enthusiasm from people we'd never seen that I was beginning to wonder what kind of strange beings we had fallen amongst.

The services were unlike anything we'd ever attended. People sang with uninhibited joy, clapped their hands, and actually raised their arms while they were singing.

Both Dick and I felt very much out of place, but agreed there was a joy here from which we could learn something.

One very cultured and refined-looking lady kept coming up to us and saying: "Has anything happened yet?"

"No, ma'am, what do you mean?" we'd answer.

"You'll see, you'll see," she always said.

Ruth and some of the others who had invited us urged me to have a private talk with a certain lady who they said had unusual power.

They took us to meet her, and I instantly disliked her. She quoted Scripture in a way that made me feel as if she was trying to convert me. I didn't like to have Scripture quoted to me, with what seemed to be a judgmental attitude.

Still, our friends insisted that we have a talk with her, and since they'd paid our way there, I felt we ought to oblige.

We sat patiently as she told us what God had done in her life and in the lives of others that she knew. She made numerous references to the "Baptism in the Holy Spirit," and went through the Scriptures to show that the experience had been a common one for Christians in the first century.

"The Holy Spirit is still doing the same thing in many people's lives today," she said. "Jesus Christ still

31

baptizes those who believe in Him, just as He did at Pentecost."

I felt a twinge of excitement. Could it be that I could experience my own Pentecost? Could I see tongues of fire, hear the rush of wind, and speak in an unknown tongue?

She had finished talking and sat looking at us.

"I'd like to pray for you," she said softly. "That you might receive the Baptism in the Holy Spirit."

Without hesitating I said, "Yes."

She placed her hands on my head and began to pray softly. I waited for "it" to hit me. Nothing happened. I didn't feel a thing.

She went on and placed her hands on Dick's head. When she had finished praying I looked at him and he looked at me. I could tell he hadn't felt anything either. This whole thing was a fake.

The lady looked at us both with a hint of a smile.

"You haven't felt anything yet, have you?"

We shook our heads. "No, ma'am."

"I'm going to pray for you in a language you will not understand. As I pray you will receive a new language of your own."

Again she placed her hands on my head. I felt nothing, saw nothing, heard nothing. When she was through praying, she asked if I could hear or sense any words within me that I didn't understand. I thought for a minute and realized that there were in my mind words that didn't mean anything to me. I felt certain that these strange words were strictly a product of my own imagination, and I told her so.

"If you said them out loud, would you feel as if you were being made a fool of?" she asked.

"I certainly would."

"Would you be willing to be a fool for Christ's sake?" This put the whole situation in a different perspective. Of course I'd do anything for Christ, but speaking out loud such utter nonsense could mean disaster for my future. I could imagine all those people going around telling everyone that a Methodist chaplain had been praying in an unknown tongue. I might even have to leave the Army! Still, what if this was what Christ wanted me to do? Suddenly even my Army career seemed less important. Haltingly I began to speak out loud the words that were forming in my mind.

Still I felt nothing different. I did believe that Jesus Christ had given me a new tongue as a sign that He had baptized me in the Holy Spirit, yet the disciples at Pentecost had acted like drunk men. Obviously they had been overwhelmed by some feeling.

I watched Dick; his experience seemed to be the same as mine. He spoke words of an unknown language and believed in the validity of it, yet displayed no emotional reaction.

"Your experience is based on faith in a fact, not on feeling," said the lady, apparently reading our minds.

I sat in deep thought. I didn't *feel* any different, but *was* I different? I looked up; an amazing realization had just hit me.

"I once again *know* that Jesus Christ is alive!" I said. "I don't just believe, I KNOW!"

Why, of course! The Holy Spirit brings witness of Jesus Christ, says the Bible. Now I knew that to be a fact. That was the source of the new authority of the disciples after Pentecost. They didn't remember a man who had lived and died and risen again. They *knew* Him in the present tense because He had filled them with His Holy Spirit whose primary purpose is to witness to Jesus Christ!

Even as I saw the magnitude of my sin, I also saw Jesus Christ in all His splendor as my redeemer. I saw

33

Him for what I'd always known deep in my heart that He was. All of my recent nagging doubts were swept away by a wave of joyous certainty. It was glorious! Never again could I doubt that Jesus Christ was who He said He was. Never again could I commit the folly of thinking that He had been a mere man, a good man, an example for us to follow.

What a marvelous truth: Jesus Christ living in us; His power operating through us. He is the vine. His life pulsates through our beings.

We are nothing apart from Him, can do nothing in our own power.

"Thank you, Jesus!" I stood up, and as I reached my full height, something hit me! I was suddenly filled and overflowing with a feeling of warmth and love for everybody in the room.

It must have hit Dick at the same time. I saw the tears well up in his eyes, and without a word we reached out and gave each other a bear hug, laughing and crying at the same time.

I looked at the dear lady I had resented so fiercely just a short while ago, and realized that I loved her. She was my sister in Christ!

We went downstairs for lunch, and I felt an overwhelming love for everyone I saw. I had never known anything like it.

That evening Dick and I began to pray in one of the rooms. People came in to join us and soon the room was full. As we prayed, others were filled with the Holy Spirit. The hotel rang with shouts of joy as people experienced the fullness of Christ's presence.

At 2:00 a.m. Dick and I tried to go to sleep. It was no use; we were too excited.

I said: "Dick, let's get up and pray some more." We prayed another two hours for everyone we knew, and then praised God for His goodness to us.

Prison to Praise

5

His Power Within You

I returned to Fort Bragg anxious to share with everyone the wonderful thing that had happened to me. I had once wondered how an experience like this would affect my ministry. How well I remembered my own reaction to the "Pentecostal emotionalism" in the church.

Now I knew that whatever the reaction, I would not be able to keep from sharing what I had experienced.

The first day I went to our headquarters company orderly room. The First Sergeant was sitting behind his desk. He was big and rough and well known for his gruff manners.

"First Sergeant," I said, "did I ever tell you that Jesus loves you?"

To my amazement the tears began to roll down his cheeks.

He said: "No, Chaplain, you never told me anything like that."

I felt my face flush hot with shame. For over a year I had seen him several times a day and I had never told him anything about Jesus.

I walked into the hallway and met the Supply Sergeant.

"Sergeant, did I ever tell you that Jesus loves you and I love you too?"

"No, Sir, you never told me anything like that." Again I felt ashamed, and he said: "Sir, do you have a minute to talk?" We went to my office and he poured out a host of problems I had never known he had. When he was through I asked if he would like to accept Christ as his Savior. He said he would, and knelt with tears streaming down his face.

Everywhere I went, men accepted Christ. It seemed that there was a power in me that was doing the talking for me. When I started to speak to someone, I had no idea what I was going to say, but whatever came had a new power that drew men to Christ.

It was easy to serve God this way. The old tension was gone, and I could laugh. Preaching was no longer something to labor over. It became pure joy just to let His thoughts pour through me.

All Army personnel must attend a character guidance class once a month. Teaching this class as chaplains, we are not allowed to preach. As carefully as I could, I one day told the class that the God of our country is still alive and daily answers prayers. After the class a Private came up to me, and with his nose six inches from mine, rather insolently said: "You really believe all that stuff, don't you?"

"Yes, I do," I said.

"Do you mean that if you prayed now, God would answer?"

"Yes," I said, "I know He will."

"Do you think it is wrong to smoke?"

The question was an unexpected one. "For some it may be wrong, for others right," I said evasively.

"I've been smoking since I was fourteen," the Private said. "Now I smoke three packs a day, and the doctor told me this morning that if I don't stop, it will kill me."

I said: "There's no question about it; for you it is wrong to smoke."

"Then you ask your God to make me quit!"

How could I pray like that? The obvious pat answers were swirling through my head: God helps those who help themselves, or he could pray that God would help him want to quit. But that wasn't what he'd asked me.

"God," I prayed silently, "help me know what to do."

Immediately I felt a strong impression: "Pray in your new language!"

"Out loud?"

"No, just silently."

I began to pray in the language I had received at the retreat. Then I paused.

There came another impression: "Put your hand on his shoulder and pray."

I obediently put my hand on his shoulder. "Pray what?"

"Silently pray in your new language." I did. Then came the impression again: "Translate it into English."

Without thinking, I opened my mouth and out came the words: "God, don't let him smoke again as long as he lives."

What a prayer! If the man ever smoked again he'd be convinced that God didn't answer prayer. I felt utterly confused, and just turned on my heels and left.

In the days that followed, I asked God repeatedly if I had misunderstood. Would my mistake make that man disbelieve? Again and again came the impression: "Just trust me."

Trusting God apparently meant going out on a limb without anything to hold onto but faith. With new eagerness I dove into an intensive study of God's Word. If I was going to operate on faith, it would have to be faith in the integrity and very nature of God. I had to know Him, and I found that the more I read, the stronger I believed. Bible reading had never been this exciting before. From the pages rose a new knowledge of God the omnipotent who promised that we could do all things in Christ. Who said that the power within us is the same power that raised Christ from the dead!

In Ephesians 3:20-21 Paul wrote: "Now to him who by his power within us is able to do infinitely more than we ever dare to ask or imagine - to him be glory in the Church and in Christ Jesus forever and ever, amen! (J.B. Phillips translation)

Carefully, I studied Paul's instructions to the church at Corinth. He listed the various ways the Holy Spirit was known to operate through men: there were speaking in tongues, interpretation of tongues, healing, miracles, prophesying, preaching, wisdom, knowledge, faith, discernment.

How could I know what "gifts" God wanted to express through me? Had He given me any special gifts?

Again the verse from Ephesians came back to me: "He who by His power within us." No, I didn't have any gifts. All I could do was to be willing to let God operate through me.

In other words, my job was strictly that of being obedient to the impressions or urgings I felt within me. The Scripture says that He could do far more than we dare ask or imagine. Obviously, there was no way I could anticipate or know what God wanted to do.

One evening in our prayer group, I talked about God's power to heal our bodies. One lady spoke up. "Why don't you ask God to heal one of us then?"

I felt a bit shaky. Of course I knew God could and would hear prayer for the sick. But would He hear and answer me?

"Okay," I said, with a sudden release of faith. "Who wants to be prayed for?"

"I do," said the same lady. "One of my eyes has been weeping tears for several months. Medication hasn't helped. Please pray about it."

I held my breath, placed my hands on her head, and prayed, mustering all my faith to believe that God was healing her right then. When I was through, her eye was still weeping. Had I done something wrong? Again came the prompting within. "Trust Me." All right, faith means believing something you don't see. All the stories I'd read in the Bible had made it very plain; the difference between victory and defeat was always a matter of faith. God couldn't do a thing when the Israelites refused to believe. The promises in the Bible are plentiful to those who will only believe.

"Thank you, Lord," I said out loud, "for hearing our prayer."

That night the lady called me, "Chaplain, guess what happened?" Her voice was bubbling with excitement.

"Tell me!"

"I was sitting here reading when I suddenly realized that something had happened to my eye. It is completely healed!"

I was thrilled. "Thank you, Lord," I said, "I get your point. I'll do the trusting; You'll do the rest."

A local Presbyterian minister who had been filled with the Holy Spirit had been reluctant to tell his congregation. He invited a member of our prayer group to give her testimony during a Sunday evening service, and several of us in the group came along to be in prayer.

As she told how she, a Southern Baptist, had been baptized in the Holy Spirit, there was dead silence in the church. It was evident that God was speaking to the people. At the close of the service the pastor called on me to pronounce the benediction. I stood up, but instead of giving the benediction, I began to speak the very first words that came into my mind: "Everyone who wants to come to the altar and surrender his life to God, please come forward."

Dead silence! There had never been an altar call in the history of that church. Then one by one, people began to come forward, falling on their knees.

I walked over to the first one. I didn't know what to pray. I didn't know why he had come forward. I bowed my head. Within me I prayed silently: "Show me how to pray, God." I heard "Pray in the Spirit." I silently prayed in my new language.

"Now begin to translate what you have said."

"Lord, forgive this man for his drunkenness, his dishonesty in business." I was shocked at my own words. What if I had misunderstood? I could really mess things up for my minister friend.

I walked over to the next person and followed the same procedure. "Lord, forgive this man for his vile temper, his ugly disposition, and his selfish treatment of his family."

I went from one to another, and with my hands on the person's head prayed as I was prompted to pray, prayers of repentance and confession.

By the time I was through I knew I had really crawled way out on a limb in complete trust.

After the benediction the people came to me one by one. With tears of joy they said: "You prayed for exactly what I needed, but how did you know my problem?"

Days later the minister told me that the congregation had been revolutionized. Many of the people who had come forward that night were elders and officers in the church. Now the entire congregation was overflowing with enthusiasm, zeal, and joy.

I felt like shouting. I hadn't know the problems that beset the men and women of that church, but God had. He knows the heart and mind of each of us, and can speak through us in a power that will directly minister to the exact needs of every individual. If people respond, it isn't our doing, but His. If they refuse, again we do not get blamed for a failure.

Every day and wherever I went it was the same; people responding to Jesus Christ. Whenever I fell back into the habit of trying to think beforehand what I would say to someone, the results were immediate. I became tense; the power and presence of God simply didn't flow. The principle of letting go and letting God was valid. All I had to do was relax in the presence of God, letting my mind go blank and opening my mouth in faith to speak whatever God impressed on me. Always the words spoke directly to a need, always the person was wonderfully helped.

I marveled. I had been a pastor for many years and worked hard at it, yet I had never seen so much happen in the lives of so many in the short time since Jesus Christ invaded my being in the fullness of His Spirit.

Without the pressures of having to preplan and organize and research and write sermon notes, I found that I had much more time to spend in Bible reading and prayer. It seemed as if I suddenly had more energy than ever before, and I never had the frustrating experience of wasting time on projects that turned out to be ineffective.

As long as I rested in Christ, it seemed that God took my days, and every detail, every appointment, every happening began to fall into place in a perfect whole. No longer did I experience confusion and conflicts of appointments or schedules.

My only regret was that I had not discovered this experience of yielding myself fully to God many years before.

About this time, Oral Roberts came to Fayetteville. A huge tent was set up, and night after night thousands came to hear him preach and pray for the sick. I wanted to meet him personally so I found out which local minister would be in charge of the service. I went to see him and volunteered to do anything I could to help.

He was amazed that a Methodist chaplain would want to be involved. He had never been able to get anyone but Pentecostal ministers to assist before.

From the opening night, I was on the platform in uniform. I was there next to Oral Roberts as he prayed for the sick, and I saw physical changes take place as bodies were healed! What a tremendous joy!

My chaplain friends began to hint that if I continued appearing in such places and being associated with men like Oral Roberts, I might as well forget about ever "getting anyplace" in the Army chaplaincy. They were probably right, but I'd rather be obedient to God and see His power clearly demonstrated than be seeking the temporal approval of men.

The next week I was casually leafing through a list of chaplains who had been selected for promotion to Lieutenant Colonel. I hadn't been a Major long enough to be considered, but there, on the list, was my name! Later I found that the Army has the authority to promote five percent of its officers before they are eligible under the ordinary rules.

All I could think was, "Thank You, Lord, for showing me that I can trust You to look after all my needs."

Obedience sometimes meant going against the expressed wishes of the people who came to ask for help.

A young Army Lieutenant brought his wife to see me. "She would like prayer for the Baptism in the Holy Spirit," he said.

I had a most unusual feeling within. I just knew that this girl had already received this experience. She hadn't said a word since they entered my office, yet I knew this was so.

I said: "You have already received the Baptism so you don't need to be prayed for again."

"How do you know that?" She looked surprised. "I've tried to believe ever since I was prayed for."

"I know because the Holy Spirit tells me," I said. "He also says that before you stand up you will receive the evidence of speaking in a new tongue.

This was really way-out, I thought. What if nothing happened? Her faith would surely be shaken. Yet within I felt a certainty. I invited both of them to join me in a prayer of thanksgiving for what God had already done.

Before I finished, I could hear her softly praying in her new language. She was so filled with joy that she nearly floated out of the office.

One day a young Private showed up in my office. I remembered the prayer I'd prayed for him: "God, don't let him ever smoke again." He was beaming all over his face.

"Sir," he burst out, "You'll never believe what happened to me after you left."

I'd seen enough amazing happenings in the last month to believe anything.

"Yes, I'll believe," I said. "Tell me."

"When you turned and left, I laughed and thought, *This will be easy. All I have to do is smoke, and I'll prove that God doesn't answer prayer.* I went into the latrine and lit up a cigarette, took a big drag, and immediately started to vomit. I figured that was a coincidence, probably something I ate, and later that afternoon I tried smoking again. The same thing happened. For the next three days, every time I tried to smoke I vomited. Now, if I just think about smoking I feel like vomiting."

I was overjoyed. Jesus Christ promised that the Holy Spirit would be with us to guide us into all truth. I hadn't misunderstood His instructions.

A few days later the Private came back.

"Sir, would you pray one more prayer for me?"

"I surely will!"

"Please pray that God will forgive my sins and help me to accept Christ as my Savior."

Within minutes we were on our knees together and he joyfully accepted Christ.

Months later I told about this incident in the First Baptist Church of Columbus, Georgia. After the service a man came up to me and said: "I was in Admin Company of the 82nd Airborne Division when that happened. That man was going all over the company telling about the chaplain who had fixed him so he couldn't smoke!"

What a wonderful truth! Not only does God save, He means business when He says He can remold us and make us into His image. He can literally take away our old habits and hang-ups and impure thoughts and renew us from within!

I had received the Baptism in the Holy Spirit only a couple of months ago, yet it seemed I'd already lived a lifetime in this new dimension.

Now I was in for an encounter with the enemy in force. I was suddenly the victim of an unusual affliction. All my life I'd been strong as a horse in top physical condition. Now every time I exerted myself in the least, my heart began to beat rapidly. I was weak and ached all over. Reluctantly I went to bed for a week. My condition didn't improve at all. I went to the hospital to see what the medical verdict would be, and they immediately slapped me on a stretcher and hustled me off to bed. Test after test gave no clue to what ailed me. I felt wretched, weak, and in pain, and it seemed to get worse instead of better. At this rate I'd just as soon be dead. All my energies seemed depleted, and the outlook was bleak.

Then suddenly one night when I wondered if the end might be near, there was the strong impression: "Do you still trust me?

"Yes, Lord." I whispered it into the darkened room. A quiet peace began to move through me, and I fell into a deep sleep.

The next morning I felt much better. The doctors insisted I stay in bed for a while, and I was grateful for days of prayer, praise, and study.

One day I was reading one of Glenn Clark's books, and I suddenly felt the voice within me ask: "Will you now live like Jesus?"

I could only answer: "Yes, Lord."

"But what about your thoughts and desires. Are they pure?"

"No, Lord."

"Do you want them to be?"

"Oh, yes, Lord. All my life I've struggled to overcome impure thoughts and desires."

"Will you give me all your impure thoughts?"

"Yes, Lord."

"Forever?"

"Oh yes, Lord. Forever."

Suddenly it was as if a heaviness had been lifted from me, as if a mist had parted and everything looked clean and pure. The door to the ward opened and a young nurse walked through. I followed her with my eyes. She was a beautiful young nurse, and all I could think was: "What a beautiful child of God." There was not even a fleeting thought of temptation!

Back home from the hospital, I went to our prayer group and felt a strong impression to ask them to pray for me. I had always been the one to pray for others. Now I sat in the chair in the center of the group, and they prepared to pray for me. "What do you want us to ask God to do?"

I thought for a moment. "Ask God to use me more than ever," I said. They began to pray, and suddenly, in the Spirit, I saw Jesus kneeling before me. He was holding my feet and resting His head on my knees. He said: "I don't want to use you. I want you to use Me!"

It was as if a door had opened into a new understanding of Jesus. He told the disciples that they had to permit Him to kneel before them while He washed their feet. He wants to give Himself for us each moment of our lives just as completely as He gave Himself on the cross. We have nothing to give Him; we have only to receive of Him!

6

Vietnam

In 1966 I received orders to go to Vietnam with the 80th General Support Group, then stationed at Fort Bragg.

We boarded ship in San Francisco, and as we left the bay moving out to sea, I stood at the railing feeling the peace of God within me and around me. This was His will for me, I knew.

On board I immediately started a prayer group, a Bible study, and regular worship services. We spent twenty-one days at sea and each day several men accepted Christ.

The devil would frequently whisper in my ear that they were just doing it because they were going to Vietnam and their decisions weren't really honest.

Months later I had proof of how much of a liar the devil is. Many of the men who made decisions for Christ were with a unit that left us as soon as we reached Vietnam. One day I walked into their unit, and one of the Sergeants saw me. He almost exploded with joy. "Praise the Lord, Chaplain Carothers."

He told me of all the things God had been doing. Together we went to see others in the unit who had accepted Christ aboard ship, and they told me about the Bible classes they were holding and of the men they had led to Christ.

"Do you remember Lieutenant Stover?" they asked.

"Yes, I do." I remembered the afternoon he stood on deck and told me how he had been running from God all through college. He had given his life back to Christ right there and told me that as soon as he got out of the Army he would answer the call to full time ministry.

"He has started a tremendous choir and the men really enjoy singing with him."

They took me to meet the Lieutenant and we had a joyful reunion.

As soon as I arrived in Cam Rahn Bay I organized a Saturday night prayer group. Soon there were twenty-five men meeting each week. I began by challenging them to believe that God would answer our prayers if we would just believe Him.

For several weeks I asked for specific prayer requests. Finally one evening a Warrant Officer spoke up.

"Well, Sir, I sure would be pleased for you to pray for my wife. We have been married six years and she is so against religion that she won't even let us have prayer at the table. I don't think it will do much good to pray for her, but I'd be glad for you to try."

I thought this was an unusual request to start with, but I was learning that God knows His business. I asked the men to hold hands in a circle, and we began praying for our first miracle.

None of the men had ever tried believing for a miracle, but they were willing to try. I had been sharing with them all the wonderful things God had been doing in my life since I received the Baptism in the Holy Spirit.

Near the battlefront in Vietnam they were far from the distractions at home and ready to start grasping the deeper things of the Spirit.

Two weeks later the Warrant Officer came to the prayer group with a letter in his hand. Tears flowed down his face as he read the letter to us:

"Darling, you will probably find it difficult to believe what has been happening here at home. One week ago I was standing at our kitchen sink on a Saturday morning. I began to have a most unusual experience. A big white sign began flashing through my mind. On it in big black letters was the word 'REVIVAL.' I couldn't get it out of my mind. No matter what I tried to think about, the sign stayed in front of me all morning long. By noon I was really upset. I called your sister and asked her if there was a big revival sign some place in town. I thought I might have seen it. She said there was no such sign, but they were having revival at their church. 'Would you like to come?' she asked me.

I said, 'You know I never go to such things.' But the sign stayed with me and by evening it was so strong that I called your sister and asked if I could go with her. During the service an invitation was given and I went forward. I've waited a week to write you about this for I wanted to be sure that I really was giving my life to Christ. But Darling, it is true! I was baptized today, and I am thrilled! I can't wait for you to come home so we can have a real Christian home."

"Chaplain," said the officer, "do you know what time it was here when it was Saturday morning at home?"

I shook my head.

"Saturday night when we prayed for her. That's when she began to see the sign. And do you remember Sunday morning?"

"Yes, I remember." He had come forward when the invitation had been given at the close of the morning worship service. I had said that I thought he already was a Christian and he answered: "Yes, I am, Sir, but I was standing back there and got the strongest feeling that if I came forward it would somehow help my wife."

Now he looked at me, tears flowing freely. "Chaplain, do you realize what time that was back home?"

Then it dawned on me. It had been Saturday night. The night his wife accepted Christ. An electric thrill went through our prayer group. Tears rolled down many cheeks. The men were learning for themselves that God does answer prayer.

Sitting next to the Warrant Officer was a black Sergeant. I could see that he was deeply troubled. "What's wrong?" I asked.

"Sir, my wife is like his; she won't accept any kind of religion in our home. I've been realizing that if I had just a little faith two weeks ago we could have prayed for my wife too, and maybe the same thing would have happened to her."

What a coincidence! Far away in Vietnam were two soldiers with the same unusual problem. "Let's pray for your wife right now," I said with enthusiasm.

"Sir, I believe I missed my chance. I just don't have faith to pray now."

"You don't need to depend on your faith alone," I said. "Just believe in our prayers, and we will have faith for you."

We joined hands and began to pray. There was a new fervor among the men. They had begun to see for themselves that God hears and God answers.

The next morning I was in my office when the Sergeant came bouncing in with a letter in his hand and a big smile.

"Don't tell me you got an answer already," I said jokingly.

"I sure did!"

He was nearly in orbit and suddenly the words flashed into my mind: "Before they call I will answer." Could it be?

"What does the letter say?"

It was nearly a duplication of the one we had heard the night before. The Sergeant's wife also had been saved, baptized, and was already teaching a Sunday School class.

"Oh, God," I breathed, "I love You, I love You, I love You!"

One Saturday night a new officer came to our meeting. He was obviously not in sympathy with our approach to prayer.

"Chaplain, if God is actually answering prayer, why doesn't He do something important?"

"What would you consider important?" I asked quietly.

"From the first day our little son was able to stand up, he would look at his feet and cry out in pain. We have taken him to every doctor and specialist in the area. We have had special shoes, casts, braces, wrappings, and nothing helps. He is seven years old now and every night my wife has to put his feet on a pillow and rub them before he can go to sleep. Why doesn't God do something for him?"

Under my breath I asked God to show me how to pray; then I said: "We will pray and God will heal him!" I felt very certain. "You don't believe, but we do, and God will heal him. Join the circle with us and let's pray."

The men prayed with renewed hunger to see God move. Here was a third request for someone back home. I knew God had sent it.

Two weeks later another letter arrived:

Dear:

I've waited for a week to tell you about something that is almost too good to be true. One week ago I noticed that for the first time in his life, Paul didn't mention his feet once during the day. He went to sleep that night without a pillow under his feet. I wanted to write to you right away, but was afraid of raising your hopes. The next day it was the same. It's been a whole week now, and he hasn't complained about his feet hurting!"

"Chaplain, it's hard for me to believe," said the officer, struggling to hold back the tears. "But the day my boy's feet stopped hurting is the day we prayed for him!"

For months afterward, every time I saw this officer, he would raise his arms and say, "His feet don't hurt yet!"

From then on our men began to grow in faith. More and more prayers were answered. Other men came to our group to hear about the amazing things that were going on. I began to read letters and reports of answered prayers from the pulpit Sunday mornings, and daily men would wave to me and yell, "Any new miracles, Chaplain?"

Often I called back: "The greatest miracle of all; another man has accepted Christ and received eternal life!"

As the Spirit of the Lord moved among us, many men were drawn to Christ.

One Sunday morning I had given an invitation to accept Christ, and many had come forward to pray. After the service I went into my office to spend a few minutes alone with the Lord. I was preparing to leave when a Sergeant suddenly burst through the doorway and fell on his knees in the middle of the floor.

"Please, pray for me," he cried in obvious anguish.

He then began to confess sins of immorality, addiction to alcohol and drugs, neglect of his children and wife. He poured out his sorrow with tears of repentance. When he was through, I told him how God loved him and had sent Jesus Christ to die on the cross for every one of the sins he had confessed. "All you have to do is accept Christ as your Savior, and God will give you eternal life and complete pardon," I said.

"I do, I do," he sobbed, and a smile of peace and joy flooded his face as he began to thank and praise God.

Later he told me what had brought him running to my office. Earlier that morning he had walked by the chapel on his way to the post exchange. Suddenly he felt an urge to step inside. "This is crazy," he thought, "I haven't been inside a church for six years; I don't have any reason to go now." He went on to the PX, but something kept pulling him back. Finally he decided to go to the chapel where the service was just then getting underway. He sat through it all and when the congregation stood up to sing the last hymn he realized he was shaking so badly that he couldn't stand without holding on to the chair in front of him.

He was afraid that at any moment he would fall to the floor, and he felt a powerful urge to walk to the front and give his life to God.

"I just can't," he told himself and began to leave the chapel. Outside in the street his legs began to give way and he knew that he wouldn't be able to stand up much longer. A voice inside told him that now was the time. He must obey God or else God would let him die. Without waiting any longer he turned and ran back to the chapel and burst through my doorway.

One of our chaplains was a Southern Baptist. We were good friends and he loved the Lord, but he was scared to death of my emphasis on the Holy Spirit. The ideas of faith healing, casting out of demons and evil spirits, being filled with the Holy Spirit, and experiencing the gifts of the Spirit were completely strange to him. He came to one of our prayer groups and then asked to be excused from ever attending another.

He was particularly worried about the way one of us would sit in a chair in the middle of a circle while others would place their hands on him and pray that God would meet his particular needs. He had never seen this done before, and it seemed like something unchristian to him.

Through the men who kept coming to the group, he heard of things happening. Men who were discouraged, defeated, and ready to give up would ask to be prayed for. They told him how they had experienced total release from their burdens. After sitting in the chair and having others pray for them with the laying on of hands, they had been filled with a peace and joy that stayed with them. They told how Christ had become more real to them from that moment on.

Little by little, these things were affecting the chaplain. He began to realize that God works in many ways, even in ways much different from what he had seen and experienced before. Then something unexpected happened.

A chaplain in another front line unit was killed. My friend was called to take his place immediately. He felt naturally a little apprehensive and came to my office to say goodbye. Hesitantly, he confessed that the ministry through our prayer group had come to mean a great deal to him. Then he knelt on the floor with tears flowing. He took my hands and placed them on his head.

"Merlin, please pray for me the way you pray."

Quietly I began to pray for him in tongues, and as I prayed he began to be filled with joy and peace. Laughing through tears he told me how all his fears were gone. He was ready to go into the battle lines.

A few weeks later he called me to say that he had been nearly killed in a helicopter accident the first day he arrived in his unit.

"Even then I could only feel an overflowing love and trust in Jesus Christ," he said.

My unit moved north to Chu Lai and joined the Americal Division. We were now in the very thick of the battle along with the Marines. More and more I saw evidences of God's power protecting His children. When we trust Him, no power on earth can touch us unless it is God's will.

On several occasions when I was scheduled to go to certain places I felt a last-minute urge to change my plans. Later I found that each time I obeyed such an urge, I had avoided an incident that could have gotten me killed.

Once I was scheduled to hold a service on a beach for men who were unloading five-hundred-pound bombs. At the last minute I was strongly impressed to cancel the service. At the exact time and place where we would have met, an explosion set off the bombs. If we had gathered there, many of the men would have been killed.

An old friend, Chaplain Burton Hatch, was division chaplain of the Americal Division. He invited me to hold a Sunday evening service, and at the close of the service several men came forward to accept Christ. I prayed with each one of them.

The next morning one of the men came back to the chapel. He looked a mess, with clothes dripping wet and dirty and hair plastered down his forehead. But his face shone and he kept saying: "Praise the Lord; thank you, Jesus!"

Early that morning he and five others had been fully equipped with a combat assault load: hand grenades, bandoliers of bullets around their necks, and heavy flak vests. They boarded the helicopter and headed north along the coast and over the China Sea. The pilot was flying too close to the water, and a sudden large wave hit the skid of the chopper. With a mighty jerk, the helicopter tipped over and dove straight into the sea. Men were thrown in all directions.

The young soldier suddenly realized that he was under water and going down, fast. He tried to swim toward the surface and managed to get a breath of air before going under again, weighted down by the heavy equipment. He tried desperately to free himself, but couldn't. As he began to sink, he told me, he suddenly remembered that he had accepted Christ the evening before. He was ready to die and suddenly was filled with a great peace of heart and mind. It really didn't matter if he couldn't free himself from the heavy gear. Once more he came to the surface and again he sank under. The third time he came up he realized that his strength was gone and he would soon be with his Lord. At that very moment he felt the equipment slide from around him! He came to the surface and was free. He began to swim to shore and there he found that he was the only survivor.

After several months at Chu Lai I was transferred south to Quin Yahn to serve with the 85th Evacuation Hospital. Men who had been wounded only a few hours before were brought to us. Over and over I saw the power of God working. These men were ready to accept Christ. Man after man told me how he had been saved from death by a power beyond his understanding.

"What was it?" I asked.

"I can't explain it," they would say. "All of a sudden, when I knew I was going to die, I became aware of a great power surrounding me. I was then sure I was safe. I knew it was God, and that He didn't want me to die."

Often the men asked me why God had chosen to save them. I told them that He had some special purpose for their lives and He would reveal it as they listened to His voice.

I went from bed to bed talking to the boys and was often overcome with emotion. They were torn, bleeding, and in some cases, dying. But I never heard anyone complain. They were confident that the job they had been doing was important, and that for some reason they were saved from death. I saw nurses turn away in tears as they saw the strength and courage of these men. No matter how great the pain, they would grin and say, "I'm fine."

One night a nurse called me to the hospital to see an Army Major. When he saw me he began to weep. He was covered with bandages, and for ten minutes I stood there while he tried to stop the flow of tears. I wondered what the problem was. Had he been told that his legs would have to be amputated? They were covered by heavy bandages and looked as if they were badly hurt.

Perhaps he had received word that someone at home was seriously ill.

Finally the Major gained control of himself and began to tell me an amazing story.

Just a few hours earlier he had been a passenger in a helicopter. They had been hit by ground fire and crashed into the thick jungle. Six men had been scattered over the side of a mountain. When the Major came to, he realized he was injured too seriously to move. He could hear the cries of other men who were also unable to move. In the distance he could hear rifle shots. The Viet Cong were converging on the position where they had seen the aircraft go down. They were moving in to capture the Americans.

The Major suddenly realized he had reached the end. The VC would not attempt to carry out the wounded Americans. They would probably practice the cruel sport of torturing them to death.

He tried to pray, but realized he didn't know how. He had attended church all his life, but he had never really talked to God. But all at once he "felt" someone say: "Just ask and believe!"

With a burst of anguish, and in new faith he cried: "Oh, God, please help me!" He realized that for the first time in his life he had talked to God. Still, he could hear the VC move in closer.

Miles away, another Army helicopter was flying north. The pilot later told this story: He felt a sudden, overpowering urge to turn and go east. *But why?* he reasoned. His destination was north. Contrary to all military rules he made a ninety-degree turn and headed east. He then felt an even stronger urge to fly lower and slower. This was even less logical than his first urge and contrary to all rules of flying over hostile territory. He should be flying either high or low and fast. But the urge was so strong that he went down to treetop level, and somehow knew that he was looking for something. There it was! He suddenly spotted the remains of a helicopter scattered over the jungle.

He had no idea how long it had been there, but he felt compelled to check it out. The jungle was so dense that it was impossible to land. While he hovered over the treetops, a member of his crew lowered himself by means of a winch. When the crewman reached the ground he found the wounded men. One by one he secured them to the winch and raised them into the helicopter. When the last man had been lifted to safety, he secured himself and was pulled up. Just as he left the ground, the VC arrived and started firing at him. The pilot saw what was happening, and as soon as the man was clear of the trees he moved the chopper up and out.

In a few minutes the wounded men were safe in the hospital.

When the Major had finished his story he grasped my hand and said: "Chaplain, I just wanted you to come and help me thank God for His goodness to me. I'm going to serve Him the rest of my life!"

7

Rejoice!

I returned from Vietnam in 1967 and was sent to Fort Benning, Georgia. Twenty-three years earlier I had left there, a handcuffed prisoner. Now I returned as chaplain! It was hard to even remember how I had felt then.

I was assigned as Brigade Chaplain for the twenty-one Officer Candidate companies and the twenty-one non-commissioned Officer Candidate companies. What an opportunity to lead future military leaders to Christ!

It was an exciting challenge, yet I was ever aware of my own shortcomings. I had come to see God's power and presence in and around me, but I was often a reluctant vessel.

I experienced days of discouragement and knew that this was not God's will and plan for me.

I searched the Scriptures for clues. In John 17 I found Jesus praying to the Father for us, His followers. He prayed: ". . .that they might have my joy fulfilled in themselves." That's what I wanted. The joy of the Lord, not just when things were going good, but always. Jesus prayed that I might have it, then what was keeping me from experiencing it continuously?

In Matthew 25:21 I read: ". . .thou hast been faithful over a few things, I will make thee ruler over many things: enter thou into the joy of thy Lord."

So it was a matter of my entering in. I had to do it; it wasn't given me just automatically. "But how do I enter in, Lord?"

In Luke 6:23 Jesus tells us that we are to leap for joy. He even describes when we are to leap for joy: "When you are hungry. . .when men shall hate you. . .when men shall reproach you. . .when they cast out your name as evil. . .rejoice in that day, and leap for joy." I hadn't noticed that in the Bible before.

"How do you expect me to leap for joy under those circumstances, Lord?" It didn't make much sense, but the more I read my Bible, the more Scriptures I found saying the same thing. Was there a principle involved?

I read Paul's second letter to the Corinthians. In chapter 12:9-10 he says: "Most gladly therefore will I rather glory in my infirmities, that the power of Christ may rest upon me. Therefore I take pleasure in infirmities, in reproaches, in necessities, in persecutions, in distresses for Christ's sake: for when I am weak, then am I strong."

Infirmities were the very things that up till now I had not been enjoying. I didn't like it when people turned against me; I didn't like it when accidents happened and things went wrong.

But over and over again I found the words in my Bible: "Rejoice! Thank God for everything." The Psalmist continually spoke of joy in the midst of troubles. "Thou hast turned for me my mourning into dancing," says David in Psalm 30.

I was willing to try, but how?

One evening in a small prayer group, I began to laugh. I laughed for fifteen minutes, and while I was laughing I felt God speaking: "Are you glad that Jesus died for your sins?"

"Yes, Lord, I'm glad, I'm glad."

"Does it make you feel good to think of His dying for your sins?"

"Yes, Lord, it really does!"

"Does it make you feel happy to know that He has given you eternal life by His death for you?"

"Yes, Lord, it does!"

"Do you have to strain or try hard to really be filled with joy that He died for you?"

"No, Lord, I'm filled with joy."

I knew that God wanted me to understand how easy it was to be glad that Christ died for me. I could clap my hands, laugh, and sing with thanksgiving for what He had done for me. Nothing in my life was more important; nothing could give me more joy.

I continued laughing, but everything inside me had become very silent. I felt as if God was about to teach me something I'd never known before.

God said: "It really makes you glad that they took My Son and drove nails into His hands. It really makes you glad, doesn't it? It makes you glad that they took My Son and drove nails through His feet. It really makes you glad that they drove a spear through His side and the blood flowed down His body and dripped on the ground. It makes you very happy and you laugh with great joy because they did this to My Son, doesn't it?"

Everything became very silent. I didn't know how to answer.

"It makes you glad that all that was done to My Son, doesn't it?"

Finally I had to say: "Yes, Lord, it does. I don't understand it, Father, but I am glad."

For a moment I wondered if perhaps I had given the wrong answer. Perhaps I had misunderstood.

Then to my great relief I heard Him say: "Yes, my son, I want you to be glad! I want you to be glad!"

I laughed on, and the joy within me increased as I realized that God wanted me to be glad. Then everything became very quiet again, and I knew I was about to learn something.

"Now listen, my son. For the rest of your life when anything happens to you that is any less difficult than what they did to My Son, I want you to be just as glad as you were when I first asked you if you were glad Christ died for you."

I said: "Yes, Lord, I understand. For the rest of my life I am going to be thankful. I'll praise You, I'll rejoice, I'll sing, I'll laugh, I'll shout, I'll be filled with joy for whatever You permit to come into my life."

It was easy to promise to rejoice right then; I was having a wonderful time in prayer. Joy was just flowing over me and through me like a stream.

The next morning I was sitting on the edge of my bed when I heard a voice: "What are you doing?"

"I'm sitting here wishing I didn't have to get up!"

"I thought we made an agreement last night."

"But Lord, I didn't know You meant things like this!"

"Remember what I said, 'in everything.'"

I said: "But Lord, I've got to be honest with You. I've been sitting on the edge of my bed every morning for twenty years wishing I didn't have to get up. I've been thinking how wonderful it would be if I could just lie down for five more minutes."

But the Spirit said: "You are supposed to be thankful that it is time to get up."

"Lord, that's a little beyond my ability to comprehend!"

The Lord is always very patient and kind: "Are you willing to be made willing?"

"Yes, Lord, I really am."

That night I went to bed praying: "Lord, this is a rough one. You're going to have to do it for me. I'll get up anytime You tell me to, but I don't know how to be thankful that it is time to get up."

All I could hear was: "Are you willing?"

"Yes, Lord, I am."

The next morning I woke up and the first thing that popped into my mind was my right big toe. I heard: "See if you can move it." I could.

"Are you thankful that you can move it?"

"Yes, Lord."

"Now try your ankle. Are you thankful?"

"Yes, Lord."

"Now your knee. Are you thankful?"

"Yes, Lord."

"Now see if you can sit up."

"Yes, Lord, I can. But I've got to be honest with You; I still wish I could lie down and go back to sleep."

Very patiently He said: "See if you can stand up. Are you thankful? Now see if you can walk to the bathroom. Look into the mirror. Are you thankful you can see?"

"Hallelujah!"

"Are you glad you can speak and hear?"

"Yes, Lord."

Then everything became very silent. I knew again that out of the silence I was to learn something from God.

"My son, because I love you I am going to teach you to be thankful for everything. You can learn standing right there with all the things you are thankful for, or I can let you go back to bed and not let you move, see, or hear until you learn."

I jumped two feet into the air and said: "Lord, I understand! I am thankful! I will always be thankful."

The next morning, and the next, and the next, the first thing I thought when I woke up was, "Lord, I'm thankful." Never again have I been sorry it is time to get up.

Paul said, "Most gladly therefore will I rather glory in my infirmities." Getting up in the morning had been an infirmity for me. God told me to take it and reverse it from pain into joy, and when I did, the power of Christ and His joy came upon me.

I couldn't wait to share my discovery with others, but the Spirit said no; first I had to learn for myself beyond any doubt how to turn every difficult situation into joy.

I memorized and said over and over to myself the verse from I Thessalonians 5:16-18. "Rejoice evermore. Pray without ceasing. In every thing give thanks: for this is the will of God in Christ Jesus concerning you."

One day as I was nearing a stoplight, it turned amber, but I managed to get through, legally. As I did, a smile of thanksgiving came on my face. I felt the presence of God and He said: "Freeze."

So I froze with that smile on my face.

"Why are you so happy?"

"Lord, I made it through the light, thank You."

"What would you have done if the light had turned sooner, and you had to stop?"

"Lord, I probably would have grumbled a little and wished it had waited for me to get through."

"Don't you know that I control the stoplights? That I control the universe and time itself? The next time a light turns red you must be thankful. You will know it was I who made it turn red."

The next time the light turned red I pulled up and asked God what He wanted me to do with the time.

"See that man walking across the street? He desperately needs your prayers. Just sit there and pray for him."

We say we believe in God. But do we really believe that He controls every detail of our lives, or do we think He's off on more important business? Jesus said that God knows how many hairs we have on our heads. So why can't we believe that He is more intimately concerned with every detail of our lives than we are ourselves? I certainly don't know how many hairs there are on my head!

God is controlling everything and working out everything that happens for good for those who love Him (Romans 8:28).

I was beginning to trust God more, but what about Satan? Can't he sneak in and attack us against God's will?

God permitted Satan to enter into Judas to betray His Son. God permitted Satan to make Peter so weak that he denied having known Jesus. He permitted Satan to enter the hearts of the men who plotted and schemed and crucified Jesus Christ. At any moment God could have stopped them. He could have sent ten thousand angels to sweep aside every plan of Satan. But God didn't stop it. Because He knew that when all the sin and suffering passed through Jesus, it would come out as pure joy, praise, and victory.

Satan can't do a thing to us unless he first gets God's permission. Remember God allowed Satan to test Job. The only time God gives Satan permission is when God sees the tremendous potential in the thing passing through us and coming out as joy, pure joy!

When we begin to realize this, God can bless our lives. The power of the resurrected Christ is in us.

Miracles, power, and victory will all be a part of what God does in our lives when we learn to rejoice in all things.

One morning I got into my car to go to work. It wouldn't start. In the Army there is no excuse for being late to work. I said: "Okay, Lord, here I am. You must want me to learn something, so I thank You that this car won't start."

After a while someone came along and helped me get it started.

The next morning the same thing happened. "Thank You, Lord, I know You have some wonderful reason for having me sit here, so I'm going to be filled with joy, and praise You." Again I was able to get it started.

Later that day I took the car to the post garage. I told the manager my problem. He said: "I'm sorry, Chaplain, but the man who works on that kind of car has had a heart attack and is in the hospital. I hate to tell you this, but you'll have to take it to a civilian place." He had a pained expression on his face as he said it. "Chaplain, they know our mechanic is sick, and they'll really sock it to you. They've been doing that to everyone I've sent there."

As I drove toward the "civilian" garage, a voice tried to whisper to me: "Isn't it terrible that those civilians would take advantage of us Army people?"

I told that thought to go back to where it came from, and continued thanking the Lord that He had worked out this whole incident for my personal benefit. I said: "Lord, I know You are in this and I praise You for it."

I pulled in to the garage, and the manager came over with a writing pad in his hand. With a glint in his eye, he said, "Can I help you, Sir?"

I explained my problem to him, and he went through a list of things that "might be wrong."

"We can't repair that part here, so we'll have to send it to another shop. This, however, may not be the problem so we may have to do something else. It could be several different things, but we'll keep looking till we find the trouble."

"How long will it take?"

With a smile he said, "I'm sorry, Sir, but I have no idea. It just depends."

I could imagine the cash register pounding away.

"How much will it cost?"

"I'm sorry, Sir, I have no idea what it may cost."

Our post garage was right. They were ready to get everything out of me that they could. "Thank you, Lord; You had a good reason for this."

I agreed to bring the car back the next morning to leave it there until they could find and fix whatever might be wrong.

I then managed with much difficulty to get the car started. I put it in gear and began to move forward. Just then the manager quickly stepped up and grasped my arm. "Wait a minute! I've just thought of what may be your trouble. Turn off the engine!"

With that he opened the hood and began to poke around with a screwdriver. In a few minutes he said: "Now try it and see how it works."

I stepped on the starter and the engine purred away like it was new.

"Wonderful! How much do I owe you?"

"Not a thing, Sir, glad to do it."

Then the Lord again spoke to my heart: "My son, what I wanted you to know was that you never again have to worry whether anyone will overcharge you, hurt you, or mistreat you unless it is My will. Your life is in the palm of My hand and you can trust Me for all

71

things. As you continue to thank Me in all circumstances you will see how perfectly I work out every detail of your life."

"Hallelujah, Lord!" I bounced up and down on the seat for sheer joy. "Thank You, Lord! Thank You for showing me all these wonderful things."

I rejoiced, and realized that if I had grumbled and complained the entire incident would have profited me absolutely nothing. How many opportunities I had passed up to let God teach me how much He loves me! Most of us go around carrying these opportunities as heavy burdens, but God has ordained through Christ that all of these things can be revolutionized as they pass through us and come out as joy!

How glorious to know that at this very moment God wants to fill our hearts with overflowing joy. Not because of our goodness or our righteousness or our sacrifice. It depends on only one thing, on believing the Lord Jesus. On believing that if the chair collapses under me it is His will. If the coffee is too hot or the toast soggy, it is His will.

When we begin to really believe that, the power of God begins to break loose in our lives. That's what Jesus tried to explain to us when He said, "Leap for joy when they persecute you. When you are poor. When you have sorrow."

For many years I had suffered with painful headaches. I seldom complained about it; I just thanked God that I wasn't as bad off as some people. One day He said: "Why don't you try praising Me *for* the headache?"

"*For* it?"

"Yes, *for* it."

I began to lift up my thoughts in thanksgiving that God was giving me this headache as an opportunity to increase the power of Christ in my life. The headache got worse. I continued to thank God, but with every thought of praise came increased pain. I realized that Satan and the Spirit of Christ were at war. The pain reached an overwhelming state; I held on to thoughts of praise and thanks. Suddenly I was being flooded with joy. Joy seemed to pour over every cell of my body. I had never experienced such power in joy! I was certain that if I took a step I would rise clear up into the air. And the headache was completely gone!

For fifteen years I had suffered with hay fever at least six months out of the year. Many weeks were so bad that I sneezed and coughed and held a handkerchief to my nose all day long. I had taken shots, tried medicine after medicine, prayed, fasted, and prayed some more. I went to everyone I knew or heard of that would pray for me. Nothing helped.

Why did God let me suffer? Didn't He care that I felt so miserable?

My friend, Chaplain Curry Vaughn, had told me I should believe with him that God would heal me. I avoided seeing Curry when I had one of my attacks because he always kept telling me to go on believing. I had tried believing for fifteen years and didn't know what more I could do.

One day I was scheduled to speak to a noon meeting of men in a local Methodist church. As I drove into Columbus, the water started pouring out of my nose and I sneezed so hard that it was difficult to keep on driving. The thought came: "Praise Me!"

I began to think of how good God was to let me have this infirmity of the flesh. He was permitting me to have it to teach me something. It wasn't an accident of nature that I was allergic to so many things. God had planned it this way for His glory and for my good. "Thank you, Lord, for Your goodness. If You want me to have this I'll just trust You to heal me whenever You want to."

"What do you want me to do?"

"Heal me, Lord."

"Heal you or take away the symptoms?"

"Aren't they the same, Lord?"

"No, they are not."

"Okay, Lord, then just heal me and I won't pay any attention to the symptoms." With that I knew that God had showed me something new and wonderful. Every time I had prayed for healing in the past and tried to believe, I had always been defeated when the symptoms persisted. Now I knew that the symptoms meant nothing. Faith in God's promise was all I needed; then Satan could fake all the symptoms he wanted!

When I arrived at the meeting place my nose was still running like a faucet, and I was sneezing uncontrollably.

I said, "Lord, if you want me to make a fool of myself, I'm willing. I'm leaving my handkerchief here in the car and I'm going in to speak for You."

As I walked toward the church I began to feel better. When the meeting was over I suddenly realized that I had no symptoms of hay fever.

Day after day there were no symptoms. Then one evening as I was preparing to go to a prayer group, my nose started running.

I thought: "Lord, I can't go to the prayer group. Those ladies will think I've done something wrong and You've taken away my faith. They'll gather around and urge me to believe so You can heal me. But Lord, I know You've healed me so I thank You for these symptoms."

At the prayer group one of the sisters began to exhort me to believe.

"But God has healed me," I insisted.

"Then why are you sniffing?"

"I don't know, but God knows, and I'm just praising Him."

On the way home I was continuing to thank Him for running my life just as He wanted to. If He wanted Satan to get in a few licks at me He must have good reason. He had permitted His own Son to suffer for me.

"Son?"

"Yes, Lord,"

"You've been faithful. You will never again have even one symptom unless you need it for your good."

Once again I bounced up and down on the seat. Never again would I pray for healing for the same thing twice. God says, "Ask, and you will receive, that your joy may be full" (John 16:24).

8

Praise Him!

Discovering the power in praise was one of the most exciting experiences I'd ever had; yet every time I wanted to share it with someone, it was as if God was saying: "Hold it. This isn't the time."

When Ron came to see me about his problem he was the picture of misery and despair. "Chaplain, you've got to help me. When I was drafted my wife tried to commit suicide. Now I've received orders for Vietnam, and she says that if I go she'll kill herself. What can I do?"

Ron was an attorney and a member of the bar association. But he had been drafted and preferred to join the Army as a Private. Now he was obviously distraught and unable to handle the situation with his wife.

"Ron, have your wife come in to see me, and I'll see what I can do."

Sue was also a picture of misery. Her body was frail and she sat on the edge of a chair, trembling from head to foot. Tears flowed uncontrollably down her face.

"Chaplain." Her voice was barely audible. "I'm scared; I can't live without Ron."

77

I looked at her and a wave of compassion brought tears to my eyes. I knew Sue's story. She'd been adopted as a baby, was estranged from her adopted family, and had no one in the world except Ron. The two of them were very much in love and I knew that if Ron went to Vietnam, Sue would stay alone in a rented room in a strange town.

I prayed silently for wisdom to comfort her.

"Tell her to be thankful." I shook my head in disbelief. I must have heard wrong.

"Her, Lord?"

"Yes, you may begin to share with her!" I looked at Sue's tearful face and my heart sank.

"Okay, Lord, I'll trust You."

"Sue, I'm glad you came," I said, smiling with a confidence I didn't feel. "You don't have anything to worry about. Everything is going to be all right."

Sue straightened herself, wiped away her tears, and managed a trembling little smile.

I continued: "What I want you to do is to kneel here with me and thank God that Ron is going to Vietnam."

She looked at me in blank disbelief. I nodded. "Yes, Sue, I want you to thank God."

She immediately began to weep almost hysterically. I calmed her as best I could and began reading to her from the Bible the verses I had learned to trust in over the past few months.

". . .In everything give thanks, for this is the will of God in Christ Jesus concerning you. . .All things work together for good to them that love the Lord." Carefully I tried to show her the wonderful truths I had found to be real.

Nothing seemed to help. Sue believed in God and in Christ, but in her despair her belief was of no comfort. Finally she left my office crying, with no peace of mind and certainly no joy.

"Lord, have I completely misunderstood You? That girl wasn't helped a bit."

"Patience, son. I'm working."

The next day Ron came to my office. "Chaplain, what did you tell Sue? She is worse than she was before."

"I told Sue the solution to her problem and now I'll tell you. I want you to kneel down and thank God that you're going to Vietnam and that Sue is so upset that she is threatening to kill herself."

Ron didn't see my point either. Carefully we went over the Scriptures: ". . .This is the will of God concerning you."

Ron said: "Now I understand why Sue didn't understand. I don't understand either." And he left.

Two days later they came back. "Sir, we are desperate. You must do something to help us."

They were both hoping that I as chaplain would be able to put in a plea for another assignment for Ron.

Again I explained to them the only solution God was letting me hold up before them. "All things work together for good to them that love the Lord."

"If you can only believe that God is really working this thing out for the best for both of you, then all you have to do is trust Him and begin to thank Him - regardless of what the situation looks like".

Ron and Sue looked at each other. "What do we have to lose, Honey?" Ron said. We knelt and Sue prayed:

"Lord, I thank you that Ron is going to Vietnam. It must be Your will. I sure don't understand, but I'll try."

Then Ron prayed: "Lord, this is very strange to me, too, but I trust You. Thank You that I am going to Vietnam and that Sue is so upset. Thank You that she might even try to hurt herself."

I had a feeling Ron and Sue were not as convinced as I was, but I thanked the Lord that they were trying.

They left my office, and later I heard what had happened.

Ron and Sue had gone into the chapel and knelt together at the altar. There they had turned their lives and each other over to God in a deeper commitment than ever before and now Sue had the strength to pray: "God, I thank You that Ron is going to Vietnam. You know how much I will miss him. You know I don't have a father or mother or brother or sister or family of any kind. I will trust You, Lord."

Ron prayed: "God, I do thank You. I give Sue over to You. She is Yours and I'll trust You to take care of her."

With that they rose from the altar. Ron went through the chapel and headed for his unit while Sue came back to the waiting room next to my office. She needed to sit quietly and collect her thoughts. While she sat there a young soldier came in and asked for the chaplain. Sue told him that I was busy. "But if you wait a little while, I'll tell him you're here," she offered.

"I'll wait," said the young soldier. He looked distressed and Sue asked: "What is your problem?"

"My wife wants a divorce."

Sue shook her head: "It won't do much good to see *that* Chaplain," she said, but the soldier wasn't easily discouraged, and while they were waiting he took out his billfold and began to show Sue pictures of his wife and children. When he turned to the next picture Sue screamed: "Who is that?"

"That's my mother".

"That is *my* mother", said Sue, shaking with emotion.

"That couldn't be," the soldier replied. "I don't have a sister."

"It is; I know it is!"

"What makes you think that?"

When I was a little girl I happened to find a piece of paper in my parents' desk that showed I was adopted. In the upper right-hand corner was a picture of my real mother. That's her. It's the same lady."

And it was.

Further checking revealed that Sue had been promised for adoption before she was born and her natural mother had never seen her. She had no idea where Sue was and had never heard anything about her since the day she was born.

Now Sue had a brother, a real brother, and with him came a whole family.

Was it coincidence? There are more than two hundred million people in the United States. What would be the odds against that particular soldier walking in the door to my office just as Sue had made a covenant with God to praise Him for her loneliness and lack of family?

But that wasn't all. As Ron walked back into his unit, he ran into an old friend from law school who was now a legal officer.

"Hi, old buddy, where are you going?" he said as he met Ron.

"Praise God, I'm going to Vietnam," Ron answered. They talked some more, and the friend persuaded Ron to ask for a transfer so that he could work with him in the legal office.

Ron and Sue did not have to be separated. And no longer did Sue have to cling to Ron in fear of losing Him. She had come to have a joyous confidence in Jesus Christ and went about everywhere praising Him.

Later an Officer Candidate came to my office. He openly wept for a long time. "Sir, you must help me.

My wife has been asking for a divorce. Her lawyer has just sent me the papers to sign. I just can't keep on with the Officer Candidate program. I don't even want to stay in the Army. Please help me."

"I know just how to get your problem solved. Let's kneel down and thank God that your wife wants a divorce."

He didn't understand any better than Sue and Ron did. Carefully we went over the Scriptures together. At last he decided he might as well try it. We knelt together and he prayed, turning the whole situation over to God and thanking Him for having allowed it to happen.

When he returned to his unit he was so shaken emotionally that they gave him the rest of the day off. He went to his bed and lay there, repeating over and over, "Thank you, Lord, that my wife wants a divorce. I surely don't understand it, but Your Word says I should thank You for all things, so I'll do it." All day long he thought the same things over and over. That night he couldn't sleep, so he went on thanking God. The next day he went through training in a daze. "Lord, You know I don't understand, but I thank You anyhow."

That evening he was sitting in the mess hall having dinner. As he was eating, it suddenly hit him. "Lord, you really *must* know what is better for me, much more than I do. I *know* all of this must be your will. *Thank* You, Lord; now I understand!"

At that moment another candidate tapped him on the shoulder and told him to come to the telephone.

In all the weeks he'd been a candidate, no one had ever wanted him on the phone.

When he lifted the receiver there was someone weeping on the other end. "Honey, can you ever forgive me? I don't want a divorce!"

A lady came reluctantly to see me. One of her friends had almost dragged her into my office. She told me that she had seriously been considering suicide, but didn't see what good it would do to talk about it.

Little by little she gave me the details. Her husband had fathered an illegitimate child by another woman. The child was being kept by her husband's parents. Every time she went to visit her in-laws, there was the child. To make things worse, the child's mother usually showed up at the same time. Even though they were having financial difficulties, her husband was sending money to his parents to help take care of his illegitimate child. She couldn't live with this constant pain inside anymore.

"Don't worry," I said to her. "You won't have to; there is a solution to your problem."

She looked up, rather surprised. "What is it?"

"Let us kneel here and thank God that your husband fathered this child." Again I went over the Scriptures on thanking God for all things. Wiping away her tears, she finally agreed to try it. We prayed, and she left the office determined to let God work out the problems in her life.

The next morning I called to see how she was doing. "Wonderful!"

"You are?"

"Yes, Sir, I got up this morning just filled with joy!"

"What happened?"

"When I got home yesterday I began to think what I could do now that I am thankful for my husband's baby. I decided that if I was really thankful, I ought to do something about it. So I sat down and wrote a check to my in-laws and told them to use it for the baby. This morning I feel absolutely glorious."

The next day I called her again, and she said: "I feel even better than yesterday."

"What have you done now?"

"I started thinking of a lady who lives near me who has a retarded child. I went to see her this morning and asked if I could help with the child. She was so amazed she didn't know what to say. I stayed and started to do what I could."

"Do you know what to do for a retarded child?"

"Yes, Sir. I have a master's degree in working with special children."

"Have you worked with children since you graduated?"

"No, Sir. This is the first child I've ever worked with."

"Now do you understand why God permitted that thing to happen in your life?"

"Yes, Sir, I do, and now I really praise Him!"

From that day on she was a changed woman. Those who knew her before said she had always looked and acted as if she was in great pain. Now they say she looks and acts as though she has discovered some wonderful secret, and people are being drawn to Christ through her radiance and joy.

Jesus didn't promise to change the circumstances around us, but He did promise great peace and pure joy to those who would learn to believe that God actually controls all things.

The very act of praise releases the power of God into a set of circumstances and enables God to change them if this is His design. Very often it is our attitudes that hinder the solution of a problem. God is sovereign and could certainly cut across our wrong thought patterns and attitudes. But His perfect plan is to bring each of us into fellowship and communion with Him, and so He allows circumstances and incidents which will bring our wrong attitudes to our attention.

I have come to believe that the prayer of praise is the highest form of communion with God, and one that always releases a great deal of power into our lives. Praising Him is not something we do because we feel good; rather it is an act of obedience. Often the prayer of praise is done in sheer teeth-gritting willpower; yet when we persist in it, somehow the power of God is released into us and into the situation. At first in a trickle perhaps, but later in a growing stream that finally floods us and washes away the old hurts and scars.

One Army wife came to me, convinced that her problem had but one solution.

Her husband had developed an excessive drinking problem and for the past several years had been an alcoholic. Often he would pass out drunk on the living room floor where the wife or his teen-age children would find him, stark naked. In this condition he'd also been found in the hallway of the apartment house where several other families lived.

In final desperation the wife decided to take the children and leave. Friends persuaded her to at least come talk to me first.

"Whatever you say, Chaplain, don't tell me to stay with him," she said. "I just can't do it."

"I don't really care whether you stay with him or not," I said. "I just want you to thank God that your husband is like he is." Carefully I explained what the Bible had to say about thanking God for all things and that if she tried it, God would be able to solve her problem in the best way.

She thought it sounded ridiculous, but finally agreed to kneel while I prayed that God would release in her enough faith to believe that He is a God of love and power who holds the universe in His hand.

At last she said, "I do believe."

Two weeks later I called her.

"I feel absolutely marvelous," she said. "My husband is a different man. He hasn't had a drink in two weeks."

"That's wonderful," I said. "I'd like to talk to him."

"What do you mean?" She sounded surprised.

"I just think it would be good if I talked to your husband about the power that is working in your lives."

"Didn't you tell him already?" She sounded puzzled.

"No, I haven't met him yet."

"Chaplain, this is a miracle," she cried out. "The day I was in your office he came home from work and for the first time in seven years he didn't go to the refrigerator for a beer. Instead he went into the living room and talked to the children. I was sure you had talked to him."

Our prayer of praise had released God's power to work in another person's life. The wife was openly crying over the telephone.

"Praise God, Chaplain," she sobbed, "Now I know God works out every detail of our lives."

A young soldier collapsed with a serious heart problem and was taken to the Fort Benning Hospital. He was released, but had to come back for frequent checkups and eventually was scheduled to go to another hospital for heart surgery. The news filled him with despair, and he began drinking. His despair increased until he decided to leave. He stole clothes from some of the men in the barracks and took off in the First Sergeant's car, which he wrecked totally.

The unhappy soldier was caught and put in the stockade to await trial. There another soldier led him to Christ. I went to see him, and he was still feeling depressed and afraid that he had messed up his life so thoroughly that he couldn't be of any use to anyone.

"Your sins are forgiven and forgotten," I said. "Don't think of your past as a chain around your neck. Thank God for every detail of your life and believe He has permitted all of these things in order to bring you to the place where you are now."

Together we searched the Scriptures for God's word on all things working out for those who love Him.

"And that doesn't just mean things that happen after you've asked God to take over your life," I said. "God is able to use even our past mistakes and failures when we release them to Him with *thanksgiving*."

He understood, and began to thank God in earnest for everything that had happened. As his trial neared, his defense attorney told him the best he could hope for was a five-year sentence and dishonorable discharge. The soldier remained undaunted and insisted that whatever happened, God had full control of his life and would work out whatever would be for his good.

The General Court-martial had a surprise ending. General Court-martial is never held unless the military authorities believe that the crime warrants severe punishment. This soldier was sentenced to six months in the local stockade and no discharge from the Army.

With Chaplain Curry Vaughan I went to visit him in the stockade. We thought we were there to encourage him; instead he encouraged us. He was filled with joy and it was catching. Soon the stockade rang with our laughter. The young soldier couldn't stand still; he laughed and ran and skipped around the visiting room.

Before we got ready to leave we asked how he was feeling. He had been scheduled for heart surgery and medically speaking was still in need of attention. He confessed that he felt very weak physically, and often his heart was troubling him. But he said: "It is wonderful. God is taking care of me."

We asked if he would like prayer for healing and he said:

"Please do; I believe God will heal me."

We placed our hands on him and believed that God, through Christ, was right there healing him. The soldier smiled radiantly and said: "I believe it is done."

A few weeks later I talked to the man's Company Commander.

"I believe it's a waste of government money to keep this man in the stockade."

"Why, Chaplain?" he said.

"He isn't the same man who stole clothes and a car and wrecked it. He's completely changed."

The Commander agreed and had the man released. A week later I asked him how he felt.

"Chaplain, I used to get tired after walking one hundred yards. Now I can run and I never seem to get tired. God has healed me."

Wherever I went I now shared what I had discovered about the power of praise. I was beginning to learn that praise was not just a form of worship or prayer, but also a way of waging spiritual warfare. Often when someone began to praise God for the problems that faced him, he found that Satan increased his attacks and the situation appeared to become worse instead of better. Many who tried the way of praise became discouraged and were unable to hold on to their belief that God was in charge.

Others simply didn't understand and refused to try praising God for unpleasant things. "It just doesn't make sense," they'd say. "I'm not going to praise God for something I just don't believe He has anything to do with. How can God have anything to do with my broken arm or my wrecked car or my husband's horrible temper? I'd be foolish to thank Him for something like that."

Of course it doesn't make sense. The question is, does it work? It didn't make much sense when Jesus said, "Leap for joy when you are hungry or poor or persecuted." Yet He very definitely told us to do just that. In Nehemiah 8:10 I read: "The joy of the Lord is your strength."

The enemy's arrows just can't penetrate the joy of someone who is praising the Lord. In II Chronicles 20 we read how a whole army was defeated when the Israelites simply praised the Lord and believed Him when He said that the battle wasn't theirs, but His.

The message is just as clear today. The battle isn't ours; it is God's. While we praise Him, He sends our enemies scurrying.

It was discouraging and sad to see those who refused to praise the Lord. My heart ached for them in their hopeless situations of suffering and misery. I asked God to give me wisdom to understand why they couldn't accept the way of praise, and also asked Him to teach me better ways of leading others to praising Him.

Nearly seven months after I first had the experience of laughing with joy in the Spirit, I went to a Camp Farthest Out Retreat. I was looking forward to a time of resting and rejoicing in the fellowship of brothers and sisters in Christ.

While I sat in the back of the auditorium during a healing service, I closed my eyes and on the screen of my inner vision God painted a picture.

I saw a beautiful, bright summer day. The air was filled with light, and I had a sense of everything being very beautiful. Up above was a heavy, solid black cloud beyond which nothing could be seen. A ladder extended from the ground up into the black cloud. At the base of the ladder were hundreds of people trying to get a chance at climbing the ladder. They had heard that above the blackness there was something more beautiful than anything a human eye had ever seen, something that brought unbelievable joy to those who reached it. As person after person tried to ascend they quickly climbed to the lower edge of the clouds. The crowd watched to see what would happen.

In a short while the person would come wildly sliding down the ladder and fall into the crowd scattering people in all directions. They reported that once they got into the blackness they lost all sense of direction.

My time finally came, and as I made my way up the ladder into the blackness it grew so intense that I could feel its power nearly forcing me to give up and slide back. But step by step I continued upward until suddenly my eyes beheld the most intense brightness I had ever seen. It was a brilliant whiteness too glorious to describe in words. As I came out above the dark cloud I realized that I could walk on top of it. As I looked into the brightness I was able to walk without difficulty. When I looked down to examine the nature of the cloud I immediately began to sink. Only by looking at the brightness could I stay on top.

Then the scene changed and I was back looking at all three levels from a distance.

"What does it all mean?" I asked, and the answer came:

"The brightest sunshine below the cloud is the light that many Christians live in and accept as normal. The ladder is the ladder of praising Me. Many try to climb and learn to praise Me in all things. At first they are very eager, but when they get into things that they don't understand they become confused and cannot hold on. They lose faith and go sliding back. As they fall, they injure other people who have been hoping to find a way to live in continual joy and praise.

"Those who make it through those difficult times reach a new world and realize that the life they once thought of as normal cannot be compared to the life I have prepared for those who praise Me and believe that I carefully watch over them. He who reaches the light of the heavenly kingdom can walk on top of difficulties no matter how dark they may seem as long as he keeps his eyes off the problem and on My victory in Christ. No matter how difficult it may seem to trust Me to work in every detail of your life, keep clinging to the ladder of praise and move upwards!"

I was half-dazed by the vision and the explanation and wondered how soon God would let me share it with someone.

At the camp I met a woman who was faced with problems of illness and family difficulties at home. She found it hard to believe that praising God was going to do any good.

Inwardly I asked for guidance, and God said, "Tell her!"

So I told her. "You'll be the first one to hear this," I said, and as she listened I could see how the heaviness literally left and her face and eyes lit up with a look of joyous expectancy.

In Ephesians, chapters one and two, I found my vision described in slightly different words by Paul:

". . .Blessed (Praised!) be the God and Father of our Lord Jesus Christ, who hath blessed us with all spiritual blessings in heavenly places in Christ: . . .he hath chosen us in him before the foundation of the world, that we should be holy and without blame. . .To the praise of the glory of his grace. . .that in. . .the fulness of times he might gather together in one all things in Christ. . .That we should be to the praise of his glory, who first trusted in Christ. . .that you may know. . .what is the exceeding greatness of his power to us-ward who believe, according to the working of his mighty power, which he wrought in Christ, when he raised him from the dead and set him at his own right hand in the heavenly places, Far above all principality and power, and might, and dominion. . .And hath raised us up together, and made us sit together in heavenly places in Christ Jesus." Jesus Christ is raised above all the powers of darkness, and according to God's word, our rightful inheritance is right there above the darkness together in Christ. The ladder is praise!

I was becoming more aware of the power of praise, but also aware of some of the enemy's snares.

At the time I began to search my Bible for insight into praise I was also led to Scriptures describing the power we have received in Christ over the forces of darkness. I had long been aware of the passage in Mark 16 where Jesus speaks of the signs that will follow those who believe in Him: "In my name shall they cast out devils; they shall speak with new tongues; they shall take up serpents; and if they drink any deadly thing, it shall not hurt them; they shall lay hands on the sick, and they shall recover."

I had prayed asking God to show me if this was all valid for me in the twentieth century, and if it was, when and how to use it.

I found that I often became uneasy when I was around certain people, and asking God, I got the strong impression that what was wrong with them was of a demonic nature.

I prayed that if I ever came face-to-face with someone like that during a prayer-session that God would tell me what to do.

An Army wife was deserted by her husband who left her with three children. In desperation she tried to kill herself. She was rushed to the hospital and her life was saved. Friends brought her to see me after she got home. She was the picture of despair. Her friends had told me that for several years they had never seen her smile. I began speaking to her about the way of praising God but soon felt compelled to stop. I looked into her eyes and suddenly sensed that there was something very wrong and very evil within her.

Within me was a sense of fear; I realized that I was actually face-to-face with evil.

"Lord," I prayed within. "I've come this far, I can't go back now, so I'll step out in faith trusting that You'll do the work."

Looking straight into the woman's eyes I spoke out loud commanding the vicious spirit to get out of her in the name of the Lord Jesus Christ and by the power of His shed blood.

Her glassy eyes suddenly cleared, and she could listen as I explained that God could work all things for good if she would only trust and praise Him.

She now was free to understand, and smiled with a beautiful radiance. Jesus Christ had broken the bondage of darkness that had threatened her life.

Chaplain Curry Vaughan, Jr., had begun to experience the power of praise in his own life. Soon after he had started praising God for his difficulties, he arrived home one evening to learn that his two-year-old daughter had swallowed a glassful of mineral spirits, a type of high-grade turpentine. She had already been rushed to the hospital. Curry jumped into his car and raced full speed to be with her. His mind was swirling with thoughts of fear and worry. He suddenly realized what he was doing, slowed the car to normal speed, and praised the Lord for what had happened.

At the hospital they pumped out his daughter's stomach, x-rayed her and told Curry that two things were bound to happen. First, she would run a high fever that night; second, there was a ninety-five percent chance that she would develop pneumonia.

Curry and his wife Nancy took their daughter home, prepared to watch her very closely as the doctors had ordered.

At home Curry took his daughter in his arms and prayed: "Heavenly Father, I know that Satan has tried to attack me once again, and I have praised You! Now I claim in the name of Jesus that Virginia will not get a fever and she will not get pneumonia." The next morning Virginia woke up as bright and chipper as ever. She had suffered no ill effects.

A successful businessman came to see me about his teen-age daughter. I knew the family and knew that their daughter had received more than the average amount of love and care, yet she had developed a violent hatred of her younger sister. She would lash out and strike her with whatever heavy object she could find.

The distraught parents had taken her to the psychiatrist for treatment, kept her on tranquilizers and prayed for years that God would help them find a solution to their terrible problem.

They realized the danger as the violent outbursts increased.

I met with both parents and challenged them to try the one thing they had failed to do.

"What is that?" they both asked.

"Thank the Lord that He has given you this child to meet your need. Really praise Him for knowing exactly what would be the greatest blessing to your family."

At first they thought this was completely beyond what they could do. They had tried for years to solve the problem, and knew of no way to suddenly be glad that everything was exactly the way it was. We went through the Scriptures together and then prayed that God would work a miracle and help them to thank Him.

A miracle did happen. They began to feel and be thankful. They practiced this daily for two weeks. Instead of constant worry and fear they experienced peace and joy.

One evening they were in the living room. Their oldest daughter stood in the middle of the floor holding a potted flower. She looked at them, and when she had their attention she smiled and dropped the pot in the middle of the rug. Dirt, glass and flowers went in all directions. The girl stood smiling, waiting for their reaction. Both parents had given themselves so completely to the practice of praising God that they automatically said, at the same time: "Thank You, Lord."

The daughter looked at them in amazement. Then she lifted her head and, looking toward heaven, she said: "Thank You, Lord, for teaching me." From that very moment she began to get well.

Her parents came to me rejoicing. The power of praise had worked. For years Satan had held the family in bondage through that girl. Now his spell was broken. In James we read that we are to draw near to

God and resist Satan. In Romans 12:21 Paul describes how: "Don't allow yourself to be overpowered by evil. Take the offensive - overpower evil with good!"

Some have asked me if this principle of praise isn't just another way to talk about the power of positive thinking. Far from it. Praising God for every circumstance does not mean we close our eyes to the difficulties. In his letter to the Philippians Paul says to worry about nothing, but "In everything by prayer and supplication with *thanksgiving* let your requests be made known to God. And the peace of God, which passes all understanding, will keep your hearts and your minds in Christ Jesus."

Looking only at the good side of every situation is often a dangerous way of trying to escape the reality of it. When we praise God we thank Him *for* our situation, not in spite of it.

We are not trying to avoid our dilemmas. Rather Jesus Christ is showing us a way to overcome them.

There is a ladder of praise and I believe that everyone without exception can begin to praise God right now in whatever situation he may find himself.

For our praise to reach the perfection God wants for us, it needs to be free of any thoughts of reward. Praise is not another way of bargaining with the Lord. We don't say, "Now we've praised You in the middle of this mess, so get us out of it!"

Praising God with a pure heart means we must let God cleanse our hearts from impure motives and hidden designs. We have to experience the dying to self so that we can live again in Christ in newness of mind and spirit.

Dying to self is a progressive journey, and I have come to believe it is traveled only through praise.

God is calling us to praise Him, and the highest form of praise is the one Paul exhorts us to give in Hebrews 13:15: "By (Christ) therefore let us offer the sacrifice of praise to God continually, that is, the fruit of our lips, giving thanks to his name."

The sacrifice of praise is offered when all is darkness around us. It is offered of a heavy heart, unto God because He is God and Father and Lord.

As we begin to praise Him, on whatever step of the ladder we may be, His Holy Spirit begins to fill our beings more and more.

To continually praise Him means a steady decreasing of self and an increase of the presence of Christ within us until with Peter we rejoice with joy unspeakable and full of glory.

And a voice came out of the throne, saying, Praise our God, all ye his servants, and ye that fear Him, both small and great.

And I heard as it were the voice of a great multitude, and as the voice of many waters, and as the voice of mighty thunderings saying ALLELUIA!

Revelation 19:5-6

If the Lord uses this book to better your life, please write an account of it in your own words and send it to:

Merlin R. Carothers
Box 2518
Escondido, CA 92025

97

On National Ten Best-Selling List for 75 weeks! This unique recognition was amplified by the fact that Merlin Carothers' first book was on the same list at the same time! Two of the National Ten Best-Selling books were by the same author.

POWER IN PRAISE

by

Merlin R. Carothers

Because it has had such dramatic impact upon its readers, this book has been translated, printed and distributed in the following languages and continues to be a best-seller.

Afrikaans		*Italian*
Danish		*Japanese*
Dutch		*Norwegian*
English		*Portuguese*
Finnish		*Spanish*
French	*German*	*Swedish*

It is also printed and distributed in:

England	*Canada*	*New Zealand*

Edited by
Jorunn Oftedal Ricketts

Unless otherwise identified, all scripture references are taken from *The Living Bible,* translated by Ken Taylor, Tyndale House, Wheaton, Illinois, 1971.

CONTENTS

BOOKS BY MERLIN CAROTHERS
Prison to Praise
Power in Praise
Answers to Praise
Praise Works!
Walking and Leaping
Bringing Heaven into Hell
Victory on Praise Mountain
The Bible on Praise
More Power to You!
What's on Your Mind?

"If anyone could tell you the shortest, surest way to all happiness and perfection, he must tell you to make it a rule to yourself to thank and praise God for everything that happens to you. For it is certain that whatever seeming calamity happens to you, if you thank and praise God for it, you turn it into a blessing..."
— *William Law, English clergyman, eighteenth century*

"I thank God for my handicaps, for through them I have found myself, my work and my God."
— *Helen Keller*

"Blessed is he who submits to the will of God; he can never be unhappy. Men may deal with him as they will... he is without care; he knows that 'all things work together for good to them that love God, to them who are called according to His purpose.' "
— *Martin Luther*

"Cry for grace from God to be able to see God's hand in every trial, and then for grace... to submit at once to it. Not only to submit, but to acquiesce, and to rejoice in it... I think there is generally an end to troubles when we get to that."
— *Charles H. Spurgeon*

1

The Power in Praise

Jim's father had been an alcoholic for thirty years. All those years Jim's mother, and later Jim and his young wife, had prayed that God would heal him, but with no apparent result. Jim's father refused to admit that he had a problem with alcohol, and stalked out in anger if anyone ever mentioned religion to him.

One day Jim heard me speak about the power that is released when we begin to praise God *for* everything in our lives instead of pleading with Him to change the circumstances that hurt us.

Jim brought home a tape of a meeting and played it over and over again for his friends. Then one day it struck him; he had never tried praising God *for* his father's condition. Excitedly he shared the thought with his wife.

"Honey, let us thank God for Dad's alcoholism and praise Him that the condition is part of His wonderful plan for Dad's life!"

For the rest of that day they gave thanks and praised God for every aspect of the situation, and by evening they felt a new sense of excitement and expectation.

The next day the parents came over for the usual Sunday dinner visit. Always before, Jim's father had cut the visit as short as possible, leaving right after dinner. This time, over a cup of coffee, he suddenly asked a pointed question.

1

"What do you think about this Jesus Revolution?" He turned to Jim. "I saw something about it on the news last night. Is it just a fad, or is something happening to those kids who were hung up on drugs?"

The question led to a lengthy and open discussion about Christianity. The elder couple didn't leave till late in the evening.

Within weeks Jim's father came to admit his drinking problem, turned for help to Jesus Christ, and was completely healed. He now joins the rest of the family in telling others what praising God can do!

"Just think," Jim said to me. "For thirty years we prayed for God to change Dad. We spent only one day praising Him for the situation and look what happened!"

The phrases "Praise the Lord!" or "Thank God!" are used so glibly by many of us that we tend to lose sight of their real meaning.

Praise, according to Webster's dictionary, means to extol, laud, honor, acclaim, express approval. To praise, then, is to give positive affirmation, expressing our approval of something. Giving our approval means that we accept or agree with what we approve of. So to praise God *for* a difficult situation, a sickness or disaster, means literally that we accept and approve of its happening, as part of God's plan for our lives.

We can't really praise God without being thankful for the thing we are praising Him for. And we can't really be thankful without being happy about whatever we're thankful for. Praising, then, involves both gratitude and joy.

The very fact that we praise *God* and not some unknown fate also means that we are accepting the fact that God is responsible for what is happening. Otherwise it would make little sense thanking *Him* for it.

"Always be joyful. Always keep on praying. No matter what happens, always be thankful, for this is God's will for you who belong to Christ Jesus" (I Thess. 5:16-18).

I've met many people who are able to praise God for their circumstances, simply because they accept the word of the Bible that they are supposed to praise God in everything. Praising Him, they soon experience the results of an attitude of consistent thanksgiving and joy; and in turn, their faith is strengthened, and they can continue to live this way.

Others find it a little more difficult.

"I just don't understand," they say. "I try praising God, but it is so hard for me to believe that He really has a hand in all the horrible things that have happened to me lately."

We say we don't understand, and some of us get stuck right there; our understanding becomes a real stumbling block in our relationship with God. But God has a perfect plan for our understanding, and when we use it His way, it isn't a stumbling block, but a wonderful aid to our faith.

"For God is the King of all the earth," said the psalmist. "Sing praises in a skillful psalm and with *understanding*" (Psa. 47:7 *Amplified Bible*).

We're not supposed to push our understanding out of the way, grit our teeth, and say, "It doesn't make sense to me, but I'll praise the Lord if it kills me, if that's the only way I can get out of this mess!"

That's not praising, that's manipulating. We've all tried to manipulate God, and it is wonderful to know that He loves us too much to let us get away with it! We are to praise God *with* our understanding, not in spite of it.

Our understanding gets us into trouble when we try to figure out *why* and *how* God brings certain circumstances into our lives. We can never understand *why* and *how* God does something, but He wants us to accept with our understanding *that* He does it. This is the basis of our praise. God wants us to understand *that* He loves us and *that* He has a plan for us.

"And we know that all that happens to us is working for our good if we love God and are fitting into his plans" (Rom. 8:28).

Are you surrounded by difficult circumstances right now? Have you been struggling to understand why they have come to you? Then try to accept with your understanding that God does love you and has allowed those circumstances because He knows they are good for you. Praise Him for what He has brought into your life; do it deliberately and with your understanding.

One couple heard me speak on praising God for everything

and went home quite disturbed. For months they had grieved over the condition of their daughter who had been committed to a mental institution and had been diagnosed hopelessly insane.

Prayer groups across the country had been asked to intercede for her, and daily the parents had pleaded with God on their knees to heal their daughter. Her condition remained unchanged.

Their initial response to the challenge that they were praising God *for* the condition of their daughter had left them distraught and unhappy.

"It would be blasphemy," said the wife, "thanking God for something so obviously evil. If we thank Him, doesn't that mean we accuse Him of deliberately hurting our daughter? It just doesn't fit in with my idea of a loving God."

"It doesn't *seem* right," the husband agreed. "But what if that speaker *is* right?"

The wife looked helplessly at her husband.

"I just don't know," she said.

"We have nothing to lose, do we?" The husband looked thoughtful. "Why don't we try it?"

They knelt together.

"Dear God," the husband began, "we know that you love us and that you love our daughter even more than we do. We're going to trust that you're working out in her life what you know is best for her; so we thank you for her sickness, thank you that she's in the hospital, thank you for the doctors who haven't found a way to help her. We praise you God for your wisdom and love toward us . . ."

The longer they prayed that day, the more they became convinced that God was indeed doing what was best.

The next morning the hospital psychiatrist called.

"Sir, there's been a remarkable change in your daughter," he said. "I suggest you come and see her."

Within two weeks she was released from the hospital.

A year later a young man came up to me after a meeting. He introduced himself as the girl's brother and told me that she was married, expecting a baby, and "is the happiest girl in the world!"

A mother came and wanted prayer for her daughter who was

4

a go-go dancer in a nightclub. I told her I would be glad to pray with her and thank God for her daughter's situation. She looked at me in horror.

Don't tell me I'm supposed to thank God that my daughter mocks common decency and laughs at religion. Surely I've got the devil to thank for her misery, not a loving God!''

The mother was faced with a difficult choice. All her life she had been conditioned to thank God for everything good and blame the devil for everything bad. Together we searched the pages of my Bible for verses stating that God is able to work all things for good for those who love and trust Him, and that he wants us to be thankful in everything, regardless of how evil our situation appears.

"You can go on thinking that your daughter's situation is controlled by the devil — and by your lack of faith in God's supreme power make it difficult for Him to work out His perfect plan for her, or you can believe that God is at work, thank Him for everything and thereby release His power to work in her life."

At last the mother agreed to try.

"I don't understand why it has to be this way," she said, "But I am going to trust that God knows what He's doing, and I'm going to thank Him for it."

We prayed together, and the mother went away with a new peace in her heart about the whole situation.

"For the first time, I'm not worried at all about my daughter," she beamed.

Later she told me what happened.

That same night her daughter was dancing nearly nude on her little platform when a young man came into the nightclub. He walked up to the girl, looked straight at her and said, "Jesus really loves you!"

The go-go dancer was used to hearing all kinds of remarks from young men, but never anything like this. She came down from her platform, sat down with the young man at a table and asked, "Why did you say that?"

He explained that he happened to be walking down the street when he felt that God was urging him to go into that particular nightclub and tell the go-go dancer that Jesus Christ was offering her the free gift of eternal life.

Stunned, the girl stared at him; then tears filled her eyes, and quietly she said, "I'd like to receive that gift."

And she did, right there at the table in the nightclub.

Praising God is not a patent medicine, a cure-all, or a magic formula for success. It is a way of life that is solidly backed up in God's Word. We praise God, not for the expected results, but for the situation just as it is.

As long as we praise God with an eye secretly looking for the expected results, we're only kidding ourselves, and we can be certain that nothing will happen to change us or our situation.

Praise is based on a total and joyful acceptance of the present as part of God's loving, perfect will for us. Praise is not based on what we think or hope will happen in the future. This is an absolute "law," clearly observable in the practice of praise.

We praise God, not for what we expect will happen in or around us, but we praise Him for what He is and where and how we are *right now!*

It is, of course, a fact that when we honestly praise God, something *does* happen as a result. His power obviously flows into the situation, and we will notice, sooner or later, a change in us or around us. The change may be that we come to experience a real joy and happiness in the midst of what once appeared to be a miserable situation, or the situation may change. But this is a *result* of praise, and must not be the motivation for praise.

Praise is not a bargaining position. We don't say, "I'll praise you so that you can bless me, Lord."

To praise God is to delight ourselves in Him, and the psalmist wrote, "Be delighted with the Lord. Then he will give you all your heart's desires" (Psa. 37:4).

Notice the order of importance here. We don't make a list of our heart's desires and then delight ourselves in the Lord in order to get them. We're first to be delighted, and once we've experienced being really delighted with God, we'll discover that everything else becomes secondary. Still, it is true that God does want to give us all our heart's desires. Nothing short of that is His wish and plan for us.

6

If we could only learn to be delighted with the Lord in everything first!

A Christian couple had two sons. One was their pride and joy; he lived at home and shared his parent's warm and happy Christian faith.

Once when I was having dinner with them, they confided in me that their older son was a rebel and gone from home. He had graduated from college with honors, but had turned his back on his parents and on established society. Now he roamed the country as a hippie, with no apparent objectives in life.

The unhappy parents asked if I had any advice for them. I explained that I believed that God had given them this son and was answering their prayers for his salvation.

"If your prayers are sincere, then you can be sure that his present life is exactly what God knows is best for him, and for you!" I said.

"I understand, " said the father. "We want only what is best for our boy, and this must be God's way and will for all of us."

We joined hands around the dinner table and thanked God for working out His plan in the way He knew was best. Afterward the parents felt a great release and a new peace.

A short time later the family wrote me. Since our meeting, the parents had persisted in thanking God for their son's way of life, even if they found it hard to understand. Then one day their son had an accident on his bike and received a painful injury to his foot.

Temporarily crippled, he decided to come home for a while. He informed his parents that he'd left a trail of unpaid bills across the country. The parents prayed about it and decided that if God had really been at work in all the events in their son's life, He had also allowed the bills. So they thanked Him for every one of them and paid the debts in full!

Their son was amazed. He had expected to be reprimanded and told to take care of his own obligations. Instead, his parents were relaxed, loving, and appeared to accept his way-out style of dress and hair without cringing.

One evening some young Christians came to visit the younger

son. The older brother was obviously irritated by the intrusion, but his painful foot kept him from leaving the house. Enthusiastically, the young Christians shared what Jesus Christ had done and was doing in their lives. At first the older brother offered scathing criticism of what he called their naive and unrealistic approach to life, but soon he was listening attentively and asking probing questions. Before the evening was over, he had turned his life over to Jesus Christ.

His parents joyfully wrote that there was an immediate and drastic change in their older son's life. He dedicated himself to follow Jesus and serve Him. Eagerly he studied the Bible, and within a few days he asked for and received the baptism in the Holy Spirit, the experience the followers of Jesus had received on the first Pentecost after Christ's death and resurrection. A few days later he met a Christian girl. Two weeks later they were engaged to be married.

Months of anxious and concerned prayers had not brought a change in this young man. Only when the parents turned to God in joyful acceptance of the present conditions of their son's life was the door opened for God to complete His perfect plan for all of them.

God does have a perfect plan for your life and for mine. We may look at the circumstances surrounding us and think we've been standing still forever in one painful spot. The more we pray and cry for God to help us, the more the circumstances seem to pile up. The turning point cannot come until we begin to praise God *for* our situation instead of crying for Him to take it all away.

A young woman wrote and told me how she had reached the end of her rope. Certain embarrassing personal circumstances had caused her to lose her self-respect, and she began to neglect her looks.

"Eating was my way out," she wrote, "and soon pounds began to pile up all over my body till I looked like a three-ring circus. My husband began looking at other women, and one day he moved out, asking for a divorce.

Bills began to accumulate, her nerves were stretched to the breaking point, and the thought of suicide became more and more frequent.

"All this time I prayed continually," she wrote. "I read my Bible, went to church every time the doors were open, and asked everyone I knew to pray for me. My Christian friends kept telling me to 'keep the faith; don't let it get you down; things will be better tomorrow.' But everything kept getting worse. Then someone gave me *Prison to Praise,* I read it, and at first I couldn't believe you were serious. No one in his right mind could expect me to be thankful for everything that was going on in my life right then! But the longer I read, the more I cried. Slowly it dawned on me that what you said was real. Those scripture verses about thanking God for everything — I'd read them in my Bible countless times and never really understood what they meant."

She decided to try thanking God for everything. After all what could she lose? She'd been gaining weight so rapidly that she knew she could suffer a serious heart attack at any time. With a faint glimmer of hope she knelt in her living room to pray.

"God, I thank you that my life is just as it is. Every problem I have has been your gift to bring me to the place where I am right now. You wouldn't have permitted any of these things to happen if you hadn't known that it was best for me. God, you really *do* love me! I mean it God, I *know* you do love me . . ."

At this point her prayer was interrupted by the dog barking loudly at the mailman. Every day the dog greeted every visitor to her house with intensive barking; that was one of many irritating little incidents that seemed to pile up to make her days miserable beyond endurance. As she got up and moved toward the door to silence the dog with the usual sharp command, she suddenly remembered, *I'm supposed to be thankful for everything.* "Okay, God, thank you for my barking dog!"

The mailman brought a letter, and she stared at the familiar handwriting on the envelope. It couldn't be! She hadn't heard from her husband for months! God couldn't have moved *that* quickly. With trembling hands she opened the letter and read, "If you are still willing, there may be a way that we can work out our problems."

God's timing had been perfect. Joyfully, this young lady was now able to believe that God was indeed working in her life for

9

good. She went on to lose weight like butter sliding off a hot plate. Her friends began to comment, "You look so good! What has happened to you? You don't look like the same person!"

The same person? Yes and no. She was the same physical being, but she now lived in a new dimension of faith, knowing that God was working in every detail of her life for good. Her husband returned and they were united. She wrote, "Some mornings I wake up hearing myself talking to God, saying things like, 'Oh God, thank you for a beautiful day. I love you!''

The turning point in her life came when she began to accept her present circumstances with thanksgiving. This is a perfect illustration of the spiritual principle at work.

God has a perfect plan for our lives, but He cannot move us to the next step of His plan until we joyfully accept our present situation as part of that plan. What happens next is God's move, not ours.

Some people would like to deny that fact. They look at the transformation taking place in the lives of people who have learned to praise God for everything, and they insist that the explanation is a simple one.

"A changed attitude brings about changed circumstances," they say. "It is simple psychology. When you stop complaining and start smiling, you feel different; others treat you differently, and your whole life can undergo a dramatic change for the better."

I will agree that the formula, "Smile and the world will smile with you; cry and you cry alone," is a reasonably sound piece of advice — up to a point. But praising God is something more than a change in our own attitude.

There is no power in our words of praise as such. There is no power in our attitude of thankfulness and joy. All the power in the situation comes from God. We need to remind ourselves of that fact frequently. It is easy to fall into the trap of thinking that *we* have the power to manipulate or change a situation simply by reciting a certain form of prayer.

When we sincerely accept and thank God for a situation, believing that He has brought it about, there is released into that situation a supernatural, divine force that brings about changes beyond what can be explained as an unfolding of natural events.

While I was serving as a chaplain at Fort Benning, Georgia, a young soldier brought his wife to my office for help. She was suffering with horrible flashbacks from LSD, and the medical doctors had been unable to prescribe a cure. Fear and pain had etched deep lines into her pretty face.

"I can't sleep," she said. "I can't even close my eyes for a minute without seeing horrible animals rushing at me."

Her husband explained that whenever his wife fell asleep from sheer exhaustion, she would begin to scream almost immediately.

"I try to shake her awake, but sometimes it takes as long as ten minutes to bring her back to consciousness, and all that time she screams with an anguish that is driving me to despair as well," he said.

I listened to their tragic story and said, "I have only one suggestion. Please kneel with me, and let us thank God that you are like you are."

They both stared at me as if they were sure I hadn't meant what I said. Carefully I explained how I had learned that God wants us to be thankful for all things.

"Everything that has happened in your life so far has served to bring you to this very point," I said. "I believe God loves you and is going to do something very wonderful for you. Now He wants you to thank Him for everything that has brought you to Him."

I leafed through my Bible and showed them the scriptures I had underlined.

They both accepted what they heard and knelt to thank God for everything in their lives, particularly for the flashbacks from drugs. I could feel the presence of God in the room.

"The Holy Spirit is making it clear that He is healing you right now," I said. I placed my hand on the girl's head and prayed, "Thank you, Lord, for healing this girl right now."

She opened her eyes and looked amazed.

"Something has happened to me. When I closed my eyes to pray I didn't see anything!"

"Jesus has healed you," I said. "Now He wants to come into your life as your Savior. Will you accept him?"

Both the girl and her husband eagerly said, "Yes!" Still on their knees, they asked Jesus to come into their lives. Then they walked out of my office rejoicing.

The girl's healing was permanent. Never again did the flashbacks return. The power of the drug over her mind had been broken by the power of God.

Medical authorities admit their helplessness in dealing with addicts who've spent years in slavery to drugs. Yet in recent years we've been hearing with increasing frequency of drug addicts who've been set free after ten, twenty, or thirty years of heavy dependency on hard drugs. They've been freed by the supernatural intervention of God in their lives.

This kind of change cannot be brought about by a new attitude or a determined effort of self-will. This is God's power at work in human lives.

Any form of sincere prayers opens the door for God's power to move into our lives. But the prayer of praise releases more of God's power than any other form of petition. The Bible gives examples which demonstrate this fact again and again.

"But thou art holy, O thou that inhabitest the praises of Israel," we read in Psa. 22:3 (KJV). No wonder God's power and presence is near when we praise Him. He actually dwells, inhabits, resides, in our praises!

A remarkable example of how God works while we praise Him is found in II Chron. 20.

Jehoshaphat was king of Judah, and one day he discovered that his little kingdom was surrounded by the powerful armies of his enemies — the Moabites, the Ammonites, and the Meunites. Jehoshaphat knew that little Judah didn't have a chance in its own might, and he cried out to God:

"We have no might to stand against this great company that is coming against us. We do not know what to do, but our eyes are upon You" (II Chron. 20:12 *Amplified Bible).*

An important step in the act of praising God is to take our eyes off the threatening circumstances and look to God instead. Notice that Jehoshaphat wasn't just closing his eyes to the threat against his kingdom or pretending the enemies weren't there.

He took careful stock of the situation, recognized his own helplessness, and turned to God for help.

We are not to be blind to the very real threats of evil in our lives. Seeing them for what they are only gives us greater cause to praise and thank God for working in them with perfect control and authority. But we are not to be preoccupied with the appererance of evil around us. See it, admit our helplessness to cope with it in our own strength, then turn to God.

God said to Jehoshaphat, "Be not afraid or dismayed at this great multitude; for the battle is not yours, but God's" (II Chron. 20:15 *Amplified Bible*).

Now that is a trememdous statement, I think. We don't have the power to deal with the circumstances of our lives, so obviously, the battle isn't ours, but God's!

"You shall not need to fight in this battle; take your position, stand still, and see the deliverance of the Lord ..."

What a promise! Now what kind of position did God want Jehoshaphat to hold while he was to stand still and watch God at work?

The next morning Jehoshaphat gave the orders to his army. "He appointed singers to sing to the Lord and praise Him in their holy [priestly] garments, as they went out before the army, saying, Give thanks to the Lord, for His mercy and loving kindness endure for ever!" (II Chron. 20:21 *Amplified Bible)*.

This scene took place right in front of the massed ranks of the enemy-armies ready to slaughter the men of Judah. Can you imagine the reaction of their captains as they saw the small band of singers coming out on the battlefield against them?

I've been a chaplain in the army for many years, and I've seen men prepare for many battles. But I've never seen a commanding general order his troops to stand still right in front of the enemy lines while a special band of singers went out ahead singing praises to God.

It sounds like a pretty farfetched idea, doesn't it? It is in this kind of situation that our understanding is most likely to balk.

"It's all well and good to praise the Lord when we're in a

tough spot," we may say, "but let's not be ridiculous. God helps those who help themselves. The least we can do is go out there and fight as valiantly as we know how. Then we'll leave the rest to Him."

But what happened to Jehoshaphat and his men?

"And when they began to sing and to praise, the Lord set ambushments against the men . . . who had come against Judah, and they were [self-] slaughtered" (II Chron. 20:22-23 *Amplified Bible*).

I think it is permissible to assume that if Jehoshaphat had decided that "he better play it safe" and had ordered his men to fight, the outcome would have been very different.

Many of us are constantly defeated by the circumstances around us because we aren't ready to accept that the battle is God's, not ours. Even when we realize our own powerlessness to cope with the enemy, we are afraid to let go and trust ourselves to God's power. This is where we've allowed our own understanding to assume the wrong position in our lives. We say, "I don't understand; therefore I don't dare believe."

God's Word makes it clear that the only way out of *that* dilemma is the step of faith on our part. Believing that God's promises are valid, accepting them, and daring to trust in them leads to understanding. The principle in the Bible is very clear here: Acceptance comes *before* understanding.

The reason for this is simple. Our human understanding is so limited that we can't possibly grasp the magnitude of God's plan and purpose for His creation. If our understanding had come before our acceptance, we'd never be able to accept very much.

Jehoshaphat would never have dared follow God's plan for the battle if he had insisted on understanding it. God's proposal and promise undoubtedly staggered and went beyond Jehoshaphat's understanding. But Jehoshaphat, we read in the account, was a man who *believed* and trusted God. With his understanding, he relied on and trusted God.

Joshua was another leader who received battle orders from God that must have staggered his understanding and challenged his willingness to accept what must have seemed absurd to many who watched.

We've all sung, "Joshua fought the battle of Jericho — and

14

the walls came tumbling down."

The city of Jericho was a fortified stronghold, and the Israelites who had wandered for forty years in the wilderness certainly didn't have the weapons or the power to take the city. But Joshua believed God when He promised to deliver the enemies of Israel into their hands.

God told Joshua to march around Jericho six days in a row. On the seventh day they were to blow their trumpets and shout. "And the wall of the enclosure shall fall down in its place, and the people shall go up [over it] every man straight before him" (Josh. 6:5 *Amplified Bible).*

Joshua trusted God, but I wonder what you or I would have thought and said if we'd been among his followers. Would we have grumbled and balked at his foolhardy suggestion? I wonder what the inhabitants of Jericho thought as they stood on the sturdy fortified walls of their city and watched the Israelites march around, carrying the Ark of the Covenant with them.

At one time I used to think that the story of Joshua and the batttle of Jericho was a mixture of myth, exaggeration, and fairy tale. But archeologists have located the ruins of old Jericho in recent years, and found ample evidence that the walls of the city did collapse at a time in history corresponding to the biblical record. The walls of Jericho *did* come tumbling down. The power of God was at work while His people showed their trust and confidence by praising Him with trumpets and shouts.

The examples of Jehoshaphat and Joshua clearly demonstrate that God wins our victories by means and principles that look utterly foolish and contradictory to our human wisdom and strategies.

We are told to trust Him, praise Him, and watch Him work. This is essentially how Jesus Christ operated during His time of ministry in Israel. He openly admitted that of Himself He could do nothing; His part was to submit to His Father's will in perfect obedience, trust, and faith, so that God's power could meet the needs of the people.

We may take a look at a couple of Jesus' prayers concerning a difficult problem.

There was the case of the 5,000 who had followed Him out

of town to hear Him preach. They were hungry. The only food available was one little boy's lunch — five loaves of bread and two fishes.

How did Jesus pray? Did He plead with God to perform a miracle?

"He looked up to heaven, and praising God gave thanks, and broke the loaves, and kept on giving them to the disciples to set before the people; and He [also] divided the two fish among [them] all. And they all ate and were satisfied. And they took up twelve . . . baskets full of broken pieces [from the loaves] and of the fish" (Mark 6:41-43 *Amplified Bible*).

Some of us may object here and say, "But that was Jesus; He *knew* what God could do. It wouldn't work for us!"

But Jesus told his followers, "In solemn truth I tell you, anyone believing in me shall do the same miracles I have done, and even greater ones, because I am going to be with the Father. You can ask him for anything, using my name, and I will do it, for this will bring praise to the Father . . ." (John 14:12-13).

Jesus said we could do *greater* things. Does that mean that God possibly has a plan concerning famines around the world and the projected food shortage that environmentalists and agricultural experts so solemnly predict?

Yes, I do believe it does. I know of several instances where people have taken God at His Word, thanked Him, and praised Him for a limited food supply, and seen it stretch to feed many more than it was originally projected for.

When Jesus was confronted with the death of Lazarus, he again prayed a simple prayer of thanksgiving. When the stone was rolled away from the grave opening where Lazarus had been buried for four days, Jesus lifted His eyes and said, "Father, thank you for hearing me" (John 11:41). Then He commanded Lazarus to come from the grave. And the man who had been dead four days walked out!

The Bible says that Jesus came to earth to make it possible for us to praise God. Isaiah the prophet foretold Jesus' coming and said that He would come "to preach the Gospel of good tidings . . . to bind up and heal the brokenhearted, to proclaim liberty to the [physical and spiritual] captives, and the opening of the prison and of the eyes to those who are bound . . . to grant [consolation and joy] to those who mourn ... the oil of joy for mourning, the garment ... of praise instead of heavy, burdened and failing spirit" (Isa. 61:1-3 *Amplified Bible*).

You may recognize your own condition on the list. Are you brokenhearted? Bound by physical limitations, sickness, spiritual limitations? In physical prison, or imprisoned by your own spiritual blindness? Are you mourning? Unable to rejoice, be thankful, or praise God? Is your spirit heavily burdened and failing?

Perhaps it is because you haven't fully accepted and understood the Good News Jesus came to bring.

Praise is an active response to what we *know* that God has done and is doing for us in our lives and in this world through His Son Jesus Christ and the person of the Holy Spirit.

If we doubt in our hearts what God has done and is doing, we cannot wholeheartedly praise Him. Uncertainty about the Good News will always be a barrier to praise. If we want to be able to praise God in everything, we need to be sure our foundation is solid and without cracks of doubt and uncertainty.

2

Hear the Good News!

If I offer you ten cents as a free gift, you probably won't get very excited about it. You may wonder why I'm doing it, and you may even laugh at me. If I give you another dime and tell you again that it is free, you may shake your head, wondering some more and if I continue giving you dimes until I've given you twenty, your interest may be stimulated, but you will still be at a loss to figure out what I am trying to prove.

If, instead of a dime, I offer you a thousand-dollar bill, I'm sure you will get excited right away; and if I increase the gift to twenty thousand, you will stare at me in amazement as you begin to realize just how fortunate you are. You may cry for joy, and you will probably want to tell someone right away about the wonderful gift you've received. What great news to share with others! As long as you live, you'll want to talk about it.

"Say, did I ever tell you about the twenty thousand dollars I was given, for free!"

God has given us many wonderful gifts. They're free for the asking. But you may only know of them as ten-cent gifts. We don't get excited over ten cents. Your heart doesn't beat faster when you think of receiving a dime. You don't cry tears of gratitude and joy when you think of God's goodness. What's wrong? Is it God's gifts? No, you are living in a ten-cent world!

19

Many church-going people think of God's gift of eternal life as a ten-cent gift. They believe they have to struggle to live a good life to keep their "free gift." Trying hard to live a good life puts them under such a continual strain that they often wonder if trying hard to be a Christian is really worth it.

No wonder they aren't very enthusiastic about sharing the Good News with anyone else. To them it just means going to church on Sunday, staying away from things that might be a lot of fun, and giving their hard-earned cash in the offering plate.

If this is your "salvation," I understand why you spend all your free evenings watching TV. And why you never think of speaking to your neighbor or to a stranger on the street about God's wonderful love for us. As far as you know, God's gift to you is only equivalent to a dime, so why should you be interested in receiving any more? Dime gifts, you can do without.

But if you received a thousand-dollar gift, you'd be hungry for more! And you would tell everyone where they could get theirs.

We all want thousand-dollar gifts. Americans spend billions of dollars every year hoping to win something for nothing. We have a built-in hunger to acquire for ourselves anything of real value.

Now I tell you that God's free gifts to us are worth more than millions of dollars. He doesn't give them only to those who meet some minimum standards of behavior; Christ has already paid the price for every gift God wants to give to us.

"God says, 'I will destroy all human plans of salvation no matter how wise they seem to be, and ignore the best ideas of men, even the most brilliant of them'" (I Cor. 1:19).

Receiving forgiveness of sin and eternal life as a free gift doesn't fit into the normal pattern of life as we know it. We've been conditioned to believe that we only get what we deserve or are willing to pay for. God's plan of giving us a totally free gift seems so impossible to us that we try to attach something to His offer.

"I'll receive His free gift if I do this or that or something else," we say.

"It is from God alone that you have your life through Christ Jesus," wrote Paul. "He was the only one who made us acceptable to God; He made us pure and holy and gave Himself to purchase our salvation" (I Cor. 1:30).

The major question for you to decide when you hear wonderful news like that is whether or not Christ had the authority and the power to give you eternal life without requiring that you do one thing to deserve it. If you think that He didn't have the power and the authority, then you must do something to get yourself right with God. You will have to strive all your life to be sure you meet His standards. But God's Word declares that no matter how hard you try, you cannot be as good as He demands. Your very effort to prove your own goodness is the same as saying that God is a liar!

"Through Christ, all the kindness of God has been poured out upon us undeserving sinners; and now he is sending us out around the world to tell all people everywhere the great things God has done for them" (Rom. 1:5), wrote Paul.

Paul had received some of the "thousand-dollar bills," and he was excited! He was determined to let the whole world know.

"This Good News tells us that God *makes us ready* for heaven — makes us right in God's sight — when we put our faith and trust in Christ to save us" (Rom. 1:17).

Paul said that *God makes us ready.* When God does it, can you depend on it being done right? Will there be any room for improvement? Are you ready to face Him at the end of this life if you are what *He has made you?*

We can't make ourselves good enough, no matter how hard we try.

"No one can *ever* find God's favor by being good enough. For the more we know of God's laws, the clearer it becomes that we don't obey them" (Rom. 3:20).

The more you learn about what is right, the more you will be aware of how unrighteous you are. Only the proud of heart feel that they have made it to some state of personal goodness. Christ is the only unselfish, sinless force in the world. Only *His presence in you* makes you any better than the most sinful person who ever lived!

"Then what can we boast about doing, to earn our salvation? Nothing at all. Why? Because our acquittal is not based on our good deeds; it is based on *what Christ has done and our faith in him*. So it is that we are saved by faith in Christ and not by the good things we do" (Rom. 3:27-28).

Paul emphasized that this doctrine of faith was nothing new. He pointed out that Abraham was never accepted by God because of his good deeds, but because of his faith.

Abraham was not a *good* man, even by the moral standards of his day. When he was going into an alien country, he knew that the people there might decide to rob him of some of his possessions, his cattle, or even his beautiful wife. So to make his journey safer, he decided to introduce his wife, Sarah, as his sister. This way, he reasoned, any dangerous male suitors would show him favors instead of trying to kill him. Sure enough, it happened as Abraham had expected. The king himself saw Sarah and wanted her for his wife. She was brought to his palace, and Abraham was bestowed with fine gifts.

Now what did Abraham do? Make plans to rescue his wife? Not at all. He simply enjoyed his good fortune. God Himself had to intervene and show the king that Abraham had been deceitful.

Would you accept Abraham as a member of your church? Consider the question carefully.

God accepted Abraham, not because he lived up to the moral standards, obviously, but because Abraham believed God. His faith was accepted as all the goodness he needed. Abraham may not be good in your eyes, but he was good in God's eyes, because he believed.

You may think more of your own goodness than you do of Abraham or of some people you know, but in God's eyes, man's sinfulness is total and complete. Degrees of goodness and badness cannot determine our salvation or our usefulness in God's kingdom. Abraham didn't earn his way to heaven by being good.

Paul wrote, "For being saved is a gift; if a person could earn it by being good, then it wouldn't be free — but it is! It is given to those who do not work for it. For God declares sinners to be good in his sight if they have faith in Christ to save them from God's wrath'' (Rom. 4:5).

We are made *good in God's sight!*

If you really believed this, would you be excited about it? Would you want to tell others how simple it is to become a Christian? Just think of it: around you are millions of people who actually believe that to become a Christian they must be good enough. And they know only too well that they can never manage to become good enough. How desperate and bleak their future must look. How they need to hear the Good News.

God's gift is free! Paul wrote, "If it is by God's kindness [we are saved], then it is not by their being good enough. For in that case the free gift would no longer be free — it isn't free when it is earned'' (Rom. 11:6).

The Good News should be proclaimed everywhere, and yet most Christians are curiously tongue-tied when it comes to talking about it.

Have you ever gone up to a stranger and asked for directions to a bus station or to Joe's Pizza Parlor? Were you scared when you did it? Did your heart pound and your tongue feel dry and swollen? Of course not. Then why do you feel that way when you think of telling a stranger what Jesus Christ has done for him?

God wants us to share the Good News with everyone. Jesus told His disciples to go out and tell the whole world what He had done for us. So who do you think wants to keep it a secret?

Yes, there is an enemy prowling around, and his favorite trick is to make us fearful of sharing the wonderful news about God's free gifts. But if we are absolutely certain of what God has done for us, if we've accepted some of His free "thousand-dollar bills," then we are going to bubble over with the news.

Some people will still worry about how good God requires us to be once we've been forgiven of our sins and have received the free gift of eternal life. Paul wrote about that to the Romans.

"Now then, the question is: Is this blessing given only to those who have faith in Christ but also keep the Jewish laws, or is the blessing also given to those who do not keep the Jewish rules, but only trust in Christ? Well, what about Abraham? We say that he received these blessings through his faith. Was it by faith alone? Or because he also kept the Jewish rules?'' (Rom. 4:9).

23

Paul draws an amazing conclusion: Abraham did not keep the law, because there was no law yet given!

It is clear then, that God's promise to give the whole earth to Abraham and his descendants was not because Abraham obeyed God's laws but because he trusted God to keep his promise" (Rom. 4:13).

God has promised us an inheritance, too, not if we're good, but if we believe Him. You may not think that God's plan is a very good solution, but it is God's solution to our problem.

The Jews kept excusing themselves and insisted that they were not sinners. Many Christians misunderstand Jesus' answer to the Jews. He insisted that the law of God was far purer than they conceived it to be. They thought they were innocent, for example, of committing adultery. But Jesus explained that if they even looked at a woman and desired her, they had already committed adultery with her. Jesus told them they could tear their eyes out to keep their mind pure. But Jesus knew the mind of man. Even if a man doesn't want to sin, there is another part of him that wants to, and so we are always faced with this inward battle.

So what was Jesus trying to tell us? That we would have to work even harder to try to keep the law? No, He only wanted to show us how much we need Him. Nearly every parable and teaching of Jesus was meant to convince us of our need for a Savior. Paul declared that faith in Christ was the only way to keep the whole law.

If you try to whip your physical being into shape and actually succeed in keeping some of His laws, what have you accomplished? Nothing. Jesus made it clear that unless you keep every law perfectly, you are guilty of breaking them all.

Christ wasn't trying to discourage you, but to encourage you! He said He would do something to deliver you from the problem.

"Christ gives to those who trust in him everything they are trying to get by keeping his laws!" (Rom. 10:4).

When Christ enters your life, you'll still keep your physical body, and with it some of your unholy appetites. But there's a big difference: "When someone becomes a Christian he becomes a brand new person inside. He is not the same any more" (II Cor. 5:17).

You may look much the same, but you *aren't* the same.

"Your body will die, because of sin; but your spirit will live, for Christ has pardoned it" (Rom. 8:10).

You've become a new spiritual being inside, because Christ dwells there through the Holy Spirit. Your old physical body will one day die, but you won't. You will live forever, with Christ.

I have talked to thousands of church-going people and asked them what they thought a man must do in order to get to heaven. I've asked the question in some of the most fundamental, Bible-believing churches in our country and heard the same answer over and over.

Ninety-nine out of every hundred have told me about the things we must *do*. Keep the commandments, go to church, give your money, don't mistreat others, etc. — a never-ending list of what *they* are trying to do.

Church-going people have heard and believed the lie that salvation depends on what *we* do. No wonder the spreading of the Good News has gone slow. Who wants to come to church, receive ten cents, and then go out to tell the world about it?

Are you still convinced that God has offered you only ten-cent gifts? Have you thought that to receive God's blessing you have to have faith — plus something?

"So if you still claim that God's blessings go to those who are 'good enough,' then you are saying that God's promises to those who have faith are meaningless, and faith is foolish" (Rom. 4:14).

Paul wrote, "But the fact of the matter is this: when we try to gain God's blessing and salvation by keeping his laws we *always* end up under his anger, for we *always* fail to keep them" (Rom. 4:15).

Does that mean God gets angry with us for trying to be good and keep His law? Of course not. He gets angry because He

25

knows *why* we're trying to keep His law. If we try to keep the law for fear that God will punish us if we don't, our efforts are worthless. If we try to keep it to deserve any of His blessings, we are striving in vain. So why should we even try to do anything good? Couldn't we just be as bad as we want, since salvation is free anyway?

Now that is of course utterly ridiculous. We should do good, but only because we love God and *want* to please Him. If we fully understand what His wonderful gifts to us are, we will respond to His love by loving Him. If you cling to the idea of trying to do good to deserve God's favor, you may *never* learn to love Him. You surely will never get excited about the "thousand-dollar bills."

"Now God has shown us a different way to heaven — not by 'being good enough' and trying to keep his laws, but by a new way (though not new, really, for the scriptures told about it long ago). Now God says He will accept and acquit us — declare us 'not guilty' — if we trust Jesus Christ to take away our sins. And we can all be saved in this same way, by coming to Christ, no matter who we are or what we have been like" (Rom. 3:21-22).

The condition is, *"if we trust Jesus Christ."* To trust in yourself to be either "good enough" or not "too bad," is exactly the opposite.

What did Jesus Christ do for us?

"God sent Jesus Christ to take the punishment for our sins and to end all God's anger against us. He used Christ's *blood* and our *faith* as the means of saving us from his wrath" (Rom. 3:25).

Both of these elements are essential. One without the other won't do the job. Christ did the doing, but that won't help us if we don't respond by believing. If we get tangled up in the "doing," we will never be free to do the believing.

"He died for our sins and rose again to make us right with God, filling us with God's goodness" (Rom. 4:25). "Sin ruled over all men and brought them to death, but now God's kindness rules instead, giving us right standing with God and resulting in eternal life through Jesus Christ our Lord" (Rom. 5:21).

Our choice is clearly between God's kindness or His just

judgment. We are offered the free gift of eternal life, and the alternative is plainly death.

I remember an attractive young army nurse stationed at a hospital in Vietnam where I was chaplain. The nurse arrived full of life and vitality, but soon her happy smile faded away. She could not bear to see the young soldiers come back from the battlefront badly wounded and in pain. She often came to my office to speak about her feelings.

"How can you say that God loves these men when He lets them suffer so?" she asked me one day.

"It would be easier if you gave your worries and concern for your patients to God and trusted Him to help them," I suggested. "God loves these wounded soldiers far more than you and I are capable of.'

The nurse shook her head.

"I can't, Chaplain," she said. "Maybe someday, but not now. It hurts too much to look at the suffering. I can't thank God for it now."

Her visits to the chaplain's office became less frequent. From the dull expression in her once bright eyes, I began to suspect that she was taking pills to fight her depression. She no longer seemed to respond to what was going on around her. She was transferred, and I lost track of her.

Just recently, I received a letter from a state reformatory for women in a midwestern state.

"Dear Chaplain:

"I've traveled many miles in the wrong direction since I last saw you at the hospital in Vietnam. I seem to have lost the decent part of myself on the way. After Vietnam I couldn't find peace of mind, and I started to drift.

"It all began while I was watching the useless deaths and maiming of young bodies in the hospital. I blamed God for it all, and now I realize that by blaming Him I cut myself off from Him and destroyed myself. Now I am not able to respond to anything or anyone. I'm just existing in a grey, feelingless void.

"I know that God is the answer. I've fought it for many years, but now I know. I've wanted to write you for some time, but I've been ashamed. I remember how good it felt to be able to talk in the chaplain's office. I didn't want to accept the answer

27

then. I hope it isn't too late. Please pray for me..."

The young nurse had turned away from the gift God held out for her. Now she had come to recognize the consequences. But think of all the suffering she must have endured.

Receiving Christ's gift of eternal life is one of the easiest things you will ever do! There is nothing difficult about it. You don't have to be clever or good — even a little child can do it!

Paul wrote, "Salvation that comes from trusting Christ... is already within easy reach of us; in fact, it is as near as our own hearts and mouths. For if you tell others with your mouth that Jesus Christ is your Lord, and believe in your own heart that God has raised Him from the dead, you will be saved" (Rom. 10:8-9).

So why do some people hesitate? What are they afraid of?

The young army nurse was afraid to trust herself to a God who could let young soldiers be killed and maimed in battle. She didn't trust God's love.

"We need have no fear of someone who loves us perfectly," wrote John. "His perfect love for us eliminates all dread of what he might do to us. If we are afraid, it is for fear of what he might do to us, and shows that we are not fully convinced that he really loves us." (I John 4:18).

God *is* love. Everything He does is love in action. Our problem is we have such a limited picture of what love is all about. We've all been hurt and disappointed by human love, the kind that rewards us and accepts us when we're good and punishes and rejects us when we're bad. But that is not like God's love at all.

The Greek version of the New Testament uses two words that we translate simply as "love." One is *philia,* brotherly love; it means a deep, instinctive, personal affection. The other is *agape*, divine love. It is the kind Paul says that husbands and wives should have for each other, and *agape* is used to describe God's love for us. It means a reasoning, intentional, deliberate, spiritual devotion. It doesn't originate in feelings or emotions; it is a deliberate act of love, originating in the will. It never changes and can always be relied on, because it doesn't depend on how lovable or deserving the loved one is.

That is how God loves us. He loves us when we reject Him, when we disobey, and when we're mean. He loves us when we've made a mess of our lives, and He is always ready to accept and forgive us and to fill us with His joy and peace.

The free gift of God's love is eternal life in Christ Jesus, and it is as near to us as our mouth and our heart. We simply accept what Jesus has done for us, believe in our heart that He lives, and tell others about it. It is so simple, yet some stop short even when they *know* what the gift is all about.

Nicodemus, a religious and devout Jew, came to Jesus one night and asked Him how he could enter the kingdom of God. Nicodemus knew that Jesus was sent of God and had the answer.

Jesus told him, " 'With all the earnestness I possess I tell you this: Unless you are born again, you can never get into the Kingdom of God.'

" 'Born again!' exclaimed Nicodemus. "What do you mean? How can an old man go back into his mother's womb and be born again?'

"Jesus replied, 'What I am telling you so earnestly is this: Unless one is born of water and the Spirit, he cannot enter the Kingdom of God. Men can only reproduce human life, but the Holy Spirit gives new life from heaven.' "

Nicodemus *knew* who Jesus was, but that wasn't enough. It is necessary also to act on what we know and to accept Jesus Christ as our personal Savior by inviting Him into our lives. When He comes in, by the Holy Spirit, we are spiritually born again. We can only communicate with God in our spirit, and so we must be born again in order to be equipped to know God. If we're not born again, we're still spiritually dead.

Paul wrote, "I have been crucified with Christ: and I myself no longer live, but Christ lives in me. And the real life I now have within this body is a result of my trusting in the Son of God, who loved me and gave himself for me" (Gal. 2:20).

Paul told the Corinthians, "Check up on yourselves. Are you really Christians? Do you pass the test? Do you feel Christ's presence and power more and more within you? Or are you just pretending to be Christians when actually you aren't at all?'' (II Cor. 13:5).

Are you really a Christian? Have you been born again?

There are many like Nicodemus in our churches today. They spend time studying the scriptures and praying daily; they attend Bible studies and prayer groups and teach Sunday School. Some are even preachers. They may have grown up in church, and call themselves "born" Methodist, Presbyterian, Lutheran, Catholic, Pentecostal, Baptist, or whatever denomination they happen to be in.

They know all *about* Christianity. They know that Jesus is the Son of God who died for their sins; they know He lives again; but they've never actually surrendered *their* lives to Him and invited Him to be Lord and Savior in *their* hearts. Thousands of people regularly attend worship services and go through all the outward forms of Christianity without ever having experienced Christ *in* their lives.

The gift of salvation and eternal life is absolutely free; you can do nothing to earn it or deserve it, but you *must* receive it before it can become yours. In love God reaches out, lovingly arranges circumstances to show us how much we need Him, and draws us to Himself.

Once a Christian sergeant brought a soldier from his platoon to my office. The soldier was facing a dishonorable discharge and a prison term for using and dealing in drugs. He'd been an addict since his early teens, and the time he spent in the army had only made matters worse. He had served in Vietnam where dope was as easy to come by as chewing gum.

"I've made a mess of my life, and it's too late to change," he said. The look in his eyes was dark and desperate.

"What about God?" I asked. "He's got the power to change you."

The soldier shrugged.

"Why should He," he said. "I've never done anything for Him."

"He loves you," I said. "He sent Jesus to take the punishment for everything you've ever done. He can heal you, too."

The soldier looked glum.

"I've heard about Jesus," he said. "I'd like to ask Him to be my Savior, but I don't think it will do any good now. I can't stop using dope no matter how hard I try. I've been a junkie too long."

"God can heal you," I said confidently. "Don't you think He is more powerful than dope?"

The soldier looked doubtful.

"Are you willing to try Him?" I asked. The soldier nodded.

"I'll try anything," he said. "I want to get out of the hell I'm in now."

"Then thank God right now for what He's going to do for you in the next few minutes, and thank Him for everything that has happened in your life to bring you to this spot!"

"Now wait a minute!" The soldier looked upset. "You mean I'm supposed to thank God for everything in my life up to now, even that I'm an addict?"

"It's your addiction that brings you to Him, isn't it?" I said. "If God heals you, forgives you, and gives you a brand-new, eternal life with Jesus, don't you think you can thank Him for everything that made you see you needed Him?"

The dark look of doubt was still in the soldier's eyes.

"Will you let me pray for you?" I asked, and he nodded.

I placed my hands on his head. "Dear Heavenly Father," I prayed. "Thank you for loving this boy and drawing Him to you. Now send your Holy Spirit to help him believe that you've been working in every dark and lonely moment of his life to bring him to Christ."

When I finished there was a new light in the soldier's eyes.

"It is very strange," he said, "but for some reason I really do believe that God has taken everything bad that ever happened to me and is working it for my good."

His eyes were moist and he bowed his head again, this time praying for himself, asking God to forgive him for his rebellion, and asking Jesus to come and take over his life.

What happened next, defies my ability to explain. I placed my hands on his head again, praying that God would heal him, cleanse his mind of all desire for dope, and fill him instead with

His love. I felt a force flow through to the young soldier. His face brightened like a child's, and tears flowed down his cheeks.

"It has happened!" he shouted. "I don't need dope anymore — Jesus lives in me!"

For the young soldier it was the moment of rebirth. He would never be the same again. He was born again, not because he *felt* the presence of Jesus, but because he made a decision to trust God.

If our relationship with God was dependent on our feelings, it really wouldn't be our choice, would it? We can't choose how we're going to feel. But we *can* choose to trust, to believe, and to have faith. We are saved by *faith*, the Bible says. But many of us have a very distorted picture of faith.

"I just don't have faith to believe," we say, and what we really mean is, "I don't *feel* sure."

Faith and feelings are *not* the same.

"Now faith is the assurance (the confirmation, the title-deed) of the things [we] hope for, being the proof of things [we] do not see and the conviction of their reality — faith perceiving as real fact what is not revealed to the senses" (Heb. 11:1 *Amplified Bible*).

Faith does not originate in our emotions, our feelings, or our senses. Faith is a matter of *will*. We decide to perceive as real fact what is *not* revealed to our senses.

To be saved by *faith,* means that we accept Jesus Christ as our Savior by an act of our will, not by our emotions or feelings. We are born again by faith, saved by faith, and that means we take God's promise that it has happened once we've accepted Christ into our hearts. We may not *feel* saved or *feel* born again, but that doesn't change the fact that we *are*.

We've talked about how easy it is to make our understanding a stumbling block to faith. It is just as dangerous to try to measure our faith by feelings. We've been confusing feeling with fact for so long that we think we *are* what we *feel*. I *feel* sick — so I must *be* sick. But our feelings are changeable and can be affected by the weather, by our diet, by our sleep, or the mood of our boss. Our feelings are a poor test of reality. When we apply them as a test of our relationship with God, we get into trouble.

Jesus said, "Pray in faith, *believing* you have received." We can't pray the prayer of faith if we insist on measuring the results by our feelings. We may discover that God's truth in the Bible often says we should do the exact opposite of what we feel.

"Love your enemies," said Jesus.

Didn't He know how we *feel* about our enemies? Sure He does. But He's telling us that we don't have to let our feelings boss us around anymore. We're free to choose to love even our enemies!

We are also free to accept God's Word as fact for us, regardless of what our emotions, our senses, our intellect, or our feelings try to tell us. Our new life in Jesus Christ is a life in *faith*. That means a life in freedom from the tyranny of our own emotions, intellect, and senses. We don't have to pay attention to them anymore!

The Bible tells us we can be saved by faith, healed by faith, justified by faith, shielded by faith, walk in faith, stand in faith, live by faith, inherit the promises of God by faith, be rich in faith, pray in faith, overcome the world by faith, praise God by faith.

Our salvation experience becomes an accomplished fact when we accept it by faith. God isn't looking at our feelings, but at the decision we made. We may be torn by doubt and feeling terrible, but as long as we accept Christ on faith, God considers the transaction done. Whatever you may feel or not feel immediately following your commitment makes no difference. God accepted your surrender of will, and you were born again by His Holy Spirit.

I'm concerned when people come to me and say, "Oh, I just *know* Jesus touched me today, because I *felt* it." The same people will come back later and say, "I'm not sure I'm saved anymore; I don't *feel* the presence of God."

Praise God when you *do* have a wonderful experience of His presence, but don't let your faith depend on how you feel. A Christian who makes emotional experiments the test of his salvation will always be torn by doubts.

One woman wrote me:

"I gave my life to Jesus Christ several years ago, but nothing

33

happened. I didn't feel anything, and as time went on I lost my hope and quit trying to keep my promise to Jesus about living for Him. Since then my life has become unbearable. I'm so depressed I'm afraid I'll destroy my marriage...I've read *Prison to Praise* and know that what I feel is a deep hunger for Christ. I've prayed for forgiveness, and I want to commit myself to Him again. I accept Jesus Christ as my personal Savior and I want very much to be a part of His kingdom. I don't feel any different yet...please pray for me, because I can't go on feeling this way much longer..."

Another letter came from a young man in a federal prison:

"I believe in Jesus Christ with what I hope to be all my heart; I received Him as my Savior two years ago. I really meant it, and I felt wonderful for two days. Then I slipped right back into my old ways. I've had moments since then when I've felt the same joy, but I can't make it last. I want to serve God, but I just can't seem to find Him. I've read *Prison to Praise* and I know I need what you wrote about. How do I find it? Do you think maybe I don't want it badly enough? How can I make myself want it more? I've made such a mess out of my life. There's no meaning, the way I'm going. I've taken many Bible courses, and I still don't seem to be getting anywhere. I so badly want to find Christ. I'll soon be leaving prison, and I want to go out in the world with His love. Please pray that I may find Him and experience the joy He promised in the Bible..."

I've received hundreds of letters just like that, and wherever I go I meet people who say they aren't sure they really met Jesus.

The reason for their doubt is always the same: "I don't *feel* anything."

They are prisoners of their feelings and have greater faith in them than in God's Word. Once we surrender to Jesus, He says about us, "I give them eternal life and they shall never perish. *No one* shall snatch them away from me (John 10:28).

How do we fight our feelings and doubts?

Paul wrote, "The only condition [for salvation] is that you fully believe the Truth, standing in it steadfast and firm, strong

34

in the Lord, convinced of the Good News that Jesus died for you, and never shifting from trusting Him to save you. This is the wonderful news that came to each of you and is now spreading all over the world'' (Col. 1:23).

When doubts and feelings come to attack our faith, God tells us to stand firmly on His Word.

One lady I know has a very practical way of doing it. When a doubt comes along, she finds a verse in the Bible that tells the truth about the matter. She copies the verse on a piece of paper, and when the doubt comes, she quotes the verse to herself.

The thought would come to her when she felt discouraged, *Are you sure God heard your prayer when you accepted Jesus Christ as your Savior?*

In her Bible she found the verse, ''And this is the confidence which we have in him, that if we ask anything according to his will he hears us. And if we know that he hears us in whatever we ask, we know that we *have obtained* the requests made of him'' (I John 5:14-15 RSV).

She copied it down, and underneath she wrote, ''On January 14, 1969, I confessed my sins and asked Jesus Christ to come into my life as Savior and Lord. I know it happened because my request was in agreement with God's plan and will for my life.''

She placed the paper by her bedroom mirror, and when the doubt came, she pointed to the paper and said out loud, ''There it is. I *know* I am born again. I *know* God has accepted me, because I accepted His Son as my Savior on that day. I never have to wonder about it again.''

When she felt guilt over a specific sin she had already confessed to God, the temptation came to doubt that she'd really been forgiven. She checked her Bible and wrote, ''If we confess our sins to him, He can be depended on to forgive us and to cleanse us from every wrong. [And it is perfectly proper for God to do this for us because Christ died to wash away our sins]'' (I John 1:9).

Underneath she wrote down the sin she had confessed, with the date and the words, ''Hallelujah, I'm forgiven!''

Gradually her doubts ceased completely.

You can fight your doubts and feelings by keeping a written, dated record of your prayer-transactions, along with a Bible verse stating God's promise.

If you've been a Christian for several years, but still have recurring doubts about your salvation or your commitment, don't let your doubts and feelings fool you any longer. Make a recommitment right now and put it in writing with today's date. Some people record important spiritual milestones in their Bibles.

The Christian life is a continuous journey in faith. It is a good idea to keep a record of the way we've gone. It serves as a useful reminder on dark days when we feel sure we haven't moved at all. Looking back, we can praise and thank God for the way He's brought us.

Our faith is built on God's fact, not on feeling. But God's promise is also that we will experience more and more of His joy and peace in our lives as we go along. Rejoice when that happens, but rejoice also when you feel dry and empty.

Your salvation is still a wonderful fact. Throw the switch of your willpower in God's direction and say, "I will to believe, God. I stand on your Word."

Do it, and discover that your old dependency on feeling will gradually fade away. You will be free to believe!

"You will know the truth," Jesus promised, "and the truth will set you free" (John 8:32).

Accept God's Word as truth — and you will be free!

3

Power Unlimited

When we give our trust over to Christ, what actually happens?

"God...has blessed us with every blessing in heaven because we belong to Christ" (Eph. 1:3).

Because we belong to Christ we are children of God. We have entered His kingdom, and all the power, privileges, and rights belonging to the children of God are ours.

Just look at all the provisions our Father in heaven has made for us — "every blessing in heaven." Not because we are worthy in our own strength, *but because we belong to Christ!*

A human baby doesn't grow by stretching himself. He doesn't have to be good to deserve his daily care. He is fed, clothed, loved, and cared for by his mother and father, simply because he is their child. They know his every need, and they provide for him. His growth comes about naturally, effortlessly, as long as the child accepts his food and gets his proper rest and exercise.

Can you imagine a human child refusing to eat and sleep, telling his mother, "I'm not ready yet, Mom. I'm over here stretching. When I've grown five inches on my own, I'll be ready to eat."

But that is exactly the way many Christians behave. God has made all the provisions; He's prepared everything we need to grow — food, rest, love, care. But we're over in the corner, struggling and stretching, trying to grow so we'll be worthy to receive.

God decided to do this for us long before you and I were born.

"Long ago, even before he made the world God chose us to be his very own, through what Christ would do *for us;* he decided then to make us holy..." (Eph. 1:4).

Wait a minute! Who is God making *holy?* Have you known anybody He's made holy yet? If not, do you think He is behind on His schedule? Has He started making *you* holy yet?

Read further: "...without a single fault..."

Do you think it is possible for God to decide to make Christians be without a single fault and fail so miserably with all the people you know?

But read on: "...*in His eyes!"* God has made us holy and without a single fault "...in His eyes." He has done a great thing for us. He has changed us "in His eyes." *He* sees us differently. He alone has the power to see the new man. Who can see through the eyes of God? No one but God Himself. He has made a new creature for His own glory and praise.

When others look at you, they may see the same old you. They are not God. You may look at yourself in the mirror and be convinced that you are not holy or without a single fault, but remember that *you* are not God.

Do you dare say that God cannot see what He wants to see? Do you care more about seeing yourself as holy, or in having God see you as holy? Thousands, perhaps millions, of Christians are trying to force themselves into a holy mold to be seen by others or themselves. When they fail, as they inevitably must, the pangs of discouragement overcome them. I've seen their unhappy faces all over the country and heard their confession of failure so often that I know what is coming before they even begin.

How did God do such a fantastic thing as to make us holy in His eyes? Paul says, "We who stand before him covered with his love" (Eph. 1:4). A blanket of love! He drops it over us and then stands back to look. What does He see? His own love!

Others may see you. You may see you. God sees His own love!

Isn't that enough to start the joybells ringing in your heart, turning your life into thanksgiving and praise?

Why did God do such a marvelous thing for us? Why indeed? "He did this because He wanted to" (Eph. 1:5), Paul stated matter-of-factly. God *wanted* to wrap us in a blanket of His love. Don't you believe that He has the right and authority to give us *anything* He wants to? Every blessing in heaven? Thousand-dollar gifts?

Why did *He* choose to do it Himself? I am convinced that this was the only way He could be sure that His work would be perfect. If He had to depend on you and me doing it right, He would never have had anything worthwhile to present to His Son. The end product was to be for God's glory and not for man's.

Paul wrote, "God's purpose in this was that we should praise God and give glory to him for doing these mighty things for us" (Eph. 1:12).

The result of placing our complete faith in what Christ does for us is glorious.

"Now we can come fearlessly right into God's presence, assured of his glad welcome when we come with Christ and trust in him" (Eph. 3:12).

Too many prayers are made with a whining, self-effacing, false humility. We don't need to apologize to God for being human. He knows all about what we're like. He has watched billions of human beings and knows all of our weaknesses. Now He wants us to believe that through Christ we have the *right* to approach Him and ask for whatever we need.

God wants to bless us with *good* things; He wants us to be happy; and this is sometimes hard for Christians to understand. I grew up in poverty and our family often received gifts of charity. I grew up resenting it when people wanted to give me things or do something for me, unless I was absolutely sure they *wanted* to do it. I wanted to earn or deserve everything I got. This carried over into my relationship with God. Somehow I wasn't able to believe that God wanted to give me anything more than my immediate needs. *After all,* I reasoned, *why should He?* My vision of God's boundless love and concern for my well-being was rather limited.

Then one day when I was stationed at Fort Benning as a chaplain, I found myself far away in another state without any means of getting back to my station in time to carry out my duties as I had promised. Bad weather had canceled the flight I had planned to travel on, and the next scheduled flight would not get me home on time. To go by car was out of the question. I was grounded, and quite unhappy about it. As long as I had been a chaplain, I had never accepted any speaking engagements that would keep me from my regular duties at the base, and now it looked as if I would have to neglect my job.

I prayed, "Lord, you know I've never been late before; I place this entire situation into your hands. I know you've got a perfect plan for me. I thank you and know that you will meet my needs."

At the meeting where I was speaking, I met an air-force pilot. He was stationed at a base nearby, and when he heard of my plight, he said, "I'm going to call my commander and see if anything can be done."

The commander responded to his request, "Why sure. I need to get in some flying time myself; I'll be glad to fly the chaplain to Fort Benning. Bring him to the base at 0600 tomorrow morning."

I spent the night as a guest in the pilot's home, and the next morning at 6 a.m. we walked onto the airfield. I felt refreshed, and rejoiced that God had met my needs. Just how abundantly He had met them, I didn't quite realize yet.

I looked all over for the plane I expected to see. A row of huge four-engine planes was lined up, but nothing that looked like it was ready to be taken up on a routine flight just to put in flying time. I expected something small and not too comfortable, just something to get me home on time. That was all I needed, I thought.

My pilot friend stopped and said, "Here it is, Chaplain, step aboard."

I looked up. Before me was the biggest airplane on the runway! It seemed to be a block long.

This can't be for me, Lord! I thought. I walked up the steps in a half-daze and followed the crew member who showed me to a comfortable seat in a large lounge. I was the only passenger, and the plane was outfitted with every possible convenience. This was no cargo or transport plane.

The commander came back to introduce himself and said he hoped I would enjoy the flight. I could only mumble my thanks; I was still overwhelmed. I knew that God had provided the plane to bring me back to Fort Benning on time, but why this huge luxury plane? Why hadn't he just picked a small, adequate plane?"

I felt very undeserving, and a quick thought that such a big plane was really a waste went through my head.

"What does it all mean, Lord?" I asked, bewildered.

"Only that I love you," came the concise answer. "I want to show you that this is how I want to provide for all my children who trust me."

"I am beginning to understand, Lord," I mused, joy welling up in me as the thoughts continued.

"I want you to tell everyone who will listen to be thankful for every detail of their lives, and I will open the windows of heaven and pour out more goodness than they can ever ask for or hope for."

"Thank you, Lord," I chuckled in my seat.

"And remember," the voice continued in my mind, "you can never deserve my blessings. You cannot work for them or earn them. I must give everything to you as a free gift, and because of my own goodness, and you must learn to understand and accept that!"

Whenever I traveled on commercial planes, I landed ten miles from my office, but the huge four-engine plane landed at Fort Benning, within a few hundred yards of where I had an appointment. As I entered the building, I looked at my watch. I had arrived *exactly* on time. Not one minute early or one minute late.

God *does* provide our needs, and He does it abundantly and free. All we have to do is ask. The very *first* free gift God wants His new children to ask for is the baptism in the Holy Spirit.

That's right. The baptism in the Holy Spirit was provided as a "first feeding" for newborn believers. They need it to grow.

The Holy Spirit comes to dwell in the new believer the

moment He accepts Jesus Christ as his Savior. He is born of the Spirit. But Jesus also told His disciples that they would have to wait until they were *baptized* with the Holy Spirit before they could be His witnesses and spread the Good News with power and authority.

The disciples waited in Jerusalem, just as Jesus had told them, and on the day of Pentecost we read that there came the sound "like a roaring of a mighty windstorm in the skies above them and it filled the house where they were meeting. Then, what looked like flames or tongues of fire appeared and settled on heads. And everyone present was filled with the Holy Spirit and began speaking in languages they didn't know, for the Holy Spirit gave them this ability" (Acts 2:2-4).

This was the beginning of the Christian church. The timid disciples of Christ were now transformed into fearless, bold witnesses; they began immediately to preach the Good News with power and authority, and the same miracles that had followed Christ, followed them.

Jesus said, "Truly, truly I say unto you, he who believes in me will also do the works that I do; and greater works than these will he do, because I go to the Father" (John 14:12 RSV).

New believers were added to the church by the thousands, and when we read the Book of Acts, we see that the baptism in the Holy Spirit usually followed immediately after their conversion. When Peter preached to the household of Cornelius at Caesarea Philippi, the Holy Spirit overwhelmed the listeners as soon as they accepted what Jesus had done for them (Acts 10:44).

When the gospel was preached in Samaria, many Samaritans accepted Jesus as their Savior, and were baptized in water.

Peter and John were sent from Jerusalem, "and as soon as they arrived, they began praying for these new Christians to receive the Holy Spirit" (Acts 8:15).

Peter and John didn't tell the new Christians to wait awhile, or to study scriptures and pray and make themselves ready. The apostles from Jerusalem were concerned that the Spirit had not yet overwhelmed the new believers, and right away, "Peter and

John laid their hands upon these believers and they received the Holy Spirit'' (Acts 8:17).

The baptism with the Holy Spirit had been promised to everyone who believed in Jesus Christ. Jesus said, '' 'If anyone is thirsty, let him come to me and drink. For the Scriptures declare that rivers of living water shall flow from the inmost being of anyone who believes in me.' (He was speaking of the Holy Spirit, who would be *given to everyone* believing in him'' (John 7:37-39).

The baptism in the Holy Spirit is a free gift. It cannot be earned. Jesus, who provided our salvation, also provided the Holy Spirit.

''I will ask the Father and He will give you another Comforter, and he will never leave you. He is the Holy Spirit,'' Jesus said (John 14:16-17).

Jesus is the One who sends the Holy Spirit; He baptizes us in the Holy Spirit.

God spoke to John the Baptist when he was baptizing in the river Jordan. ''When you see the Holy Spirit descending and resting upon someone — he is the one you are looking for. He is the one who baptizes with the Holy Spirit'' (John 1:33).

Then why do so many Christians struggle so desperately to receive the baptism in the Holy Spirit? All over the country I've seen them, sad-faced and unhappy.

''What's wrong with me?'' they say, ''Am I just too worthless, too weak? I so desperately need the power of God in my life.''

A Sunday-school teacher wrote:

''I need the power of the Holy Spirit in my life. I try so hard to become more obedient and Christlike. I thought maybe I wasn't reading enough in my Bible, and I've tried getting up earlier to read for an hour and then pray for half an hour. But I still don't see any power in my life, and I haven't been able to receive the baptism in the Holy Spirit. I've confessed every sin I can think of. I've been a Christian for twenty years, but I am so sadly lacking in Christian virtues that I sometimes wonder if I'm even saved....''

Such people are like little babies standing over in a corner trying to stretch and grow so they can eat the wonderful meal

43

that's been prepared for them. They've got miserable hunger pains, but they don't want to eat until they've outgrown their pains.

Christians in the early church had the same problem. They kept thinking they had to make themselves good enough to receive God's free gifts.

Paul wrote:

"Oh, foolish Galatians! What magician has hypnotized you and cast an evil spell upon you?...Let me ask you this one question: Did you receive the Holy Spirit by trying to keep the Jewish laws? Of course not, for the Holy Spirit came upon you only after you heard about Christ and trusted Him to save you. Then have you gone completely crazy? For if trying to obey the Jewish laws never gave you spiritual life in the first place, why do you think that trying to obey them now will make you stronger Christians?" (Gal. 3:1-3).

The Galatians had already received the Holy Spirit as a result of having trusted Jesus Christ to save them, but the temptation to think of themselves as responsible for their own Christian growth had caused them to turn from a life of faith.

Pride and a temptation to take the credit for our Christian growth lures believers at all stages of our spiritual life. Satan tempts us in two obvious ways. He may whisper, "My, you're getting spiritual! Just try a little harder, and you'll have *more* power." Or he says, "Look how weak and miserable you are! No wonder God can't trust you with more of His blessings!"

You may praise yourself for your spiritual accomplishments, or criticize yourself for your failure — it amounts to the same thing. You are placing the responsibility for your worthiness on yourself instead of on God — where it belongs.

A minister had a weakness he couldn't control, no matter how hard he tried. Finally he ended up in prison convicted of forgery. The minister was a born-again Christian; he was crushed by his own failure, and sincerely repented of his sin. He was able to believe that God had forgiven Him, but he was convinced that God could never again use him to bring others to Him.

One day a friend sent him *Prison to Praise*. There he read that God used everything, even our mistakes, for good. With new hope he dared to thank God for his own mistake and imprisonment. He wrote me, "Praise God, my life has changed completely. The old regrets, guilt, and remorse that held me bound are gone. I can praise and thank God for every detail of my life, just as it is. I never before understood the wideness and depth of God's mercy. I once thought of myself as 'good' enough to be used of Him. What a joy it is to die to my old prideful self so that Christ can live in me — and nothing but Christ!"

The minister's cell soon became a temple of praise, and other prisoners were drawn to accept Christ.

When we think of ourselves or others as good enough or not good enough to be used of God, we're falling into a dangerous trap. Jesus warned his followers, "Don't judge and criticize and condemn others, so that you may not be judged and criticized and condemned yourselves."

Only God is qualified to judge, and He has already declared that we are holy and without a single fault in His eyes when we are covered by His love.

How do we dare set up a standard to measure ourselves and others by? Only God is qualified to deal with our sins. However wrong we or others may be, that is a matter for God to deal with.

When we do judge each other, we are often completely wrong. We judge each other by our manner of dress, amount of makeup, our smoking or drinking, what kind of movies we go to.

How do you select a Sunday-school teacher? Imagine two Christians side by side. One is of average height and weight, and you know he smokes. The other weighs at least three hundred pounds; he's a mountain of a man, but he has a kind smile and never forgets to bring his Bible to church.

Now which one of the two would you choose to teach on the subject "How to develop self-discipline as a fruit of the Holy Spirit"?

Smoking is a bad habit, harmful to our health, and it speaks of a lack of self-discipline. And what about the overweight man? The Bible ranks gluttony with drunkenness and says that they both deserve the death penalty! (Deut. 21:20-21). The glutton is hastening his own death, and so is the smoker.

45

I don't recommend that you should start judging overweight people and smokers. We have no right to judge either.

When the woman caught in adultery was brought to Jesus, the Jewish leaders and Pharisees asked Jesus, "Teacher... Moses' law says to kill her. What about it?" Jesus said, "All right, hurl the stones at her until she dies. But only he who never sinned may throw the first!" (John 8:7).

Who among us qualifies to pick up stones of criticism, judging, or condemnation? Measuring our "goodness" or "badness" is just another way to try to justify our standing with God by our good works instead of by faith.

When we discuss "faith" and "works," someone usually quotes the verse, "For we are his workmanship, created in Christ Jesus unto good works, which God hath before ordained that we should walk in them" (Eph. 2:10 KJV).

Now doesn't that state plainly that we are born again to do good works for God?

But look at the two verses above that one:

"For by grace are ye saved through faith; and that not of yourselves: it is the gift of God: Not of works, lest any man should boast" (Eph. 2:8-9 KJV).

Does Paul mean that we're saved by faith, but from then on we're on our own? That doesn't make much sense, does it?

Earlier in the letter to the Ephesians Paul said that we've *been made* holy and without a single fault in God's eyes, and that we've been provided with every blessing in heaven.

So what does Paul mean? Maybe he's got a different idea of "works" from what we do.

James wrote, "What is the use (profit), my brethren, for any one to profess to have faith if he has no [good] works [to show for it]? Can [such] faith save [his soul]?...Was not our forefather Abraham [shown to be] justified — made acceptable to God — by [his] works when he brought to the altar as an offering his [own] son Isaac?" (James 2:14, 21 *Amplified Bible).*

Now what kind of good works was that? Walking up on a mountain prepared to sacrifice his only son on the altar because God told him to do it — especially since that was the son through whom God had promised to bless Abraham and give him multitudes of descendants?

James went on to say, "Can't you see that his faith and his actions were, so to speak, partners — that his faith was implemented by his deed? That is what the scripture means when it says: And Abraham believed God, And it was reckoned unto him for righteousness; and he was called the friend of God" (James 2:22-23 Phillips).

So what kind of "good works" are we supposed to do? The disciples once asked Jesus the same question: " 'What are we to do that we may [habitually] be working the works of God? — What are we to do to carry out what God requires?'

"Jesus replied, 'This is the work (service) that God asks of you, that you *believe in* the One Whom He has sent — that you cleave to, trust, rely on and have faith in His Messenger" (John 6:28-29 *Amplified Bible*).

And that is exactly what Abraham did. Abraham's "good work" was that He trusted God to keep His promises. He never wavered in his faith. And so God chose to make Abraham the father of Israel.

Jesus promised His followers that they would do even greater works than He did, and we know that after receiving the baptism in the Holy Spirit, His followers preached with power and great miracles.

Their part of the great works was to *believe*. The power to perform miracles didn't belong to them, but came from God through them because they believed.

A common misconception about the baptism in the Holy Spirit is that it somehow gives *us* power, that it strengthens us, increases *our* power and ability to work for God — that it makes *us* spiritual giants.

Nothing could be further from the truth. So what do we need the baptism for?

The baptism in the Holy Spirit is designed to *reduce* us, so that more of God's presence and power can dwell in us and flow through us.

Paul wrote, "Now glory be to God who by *his mighty power* at work *within us* is able to do far more than we could ever dare to ask or even dream of — infinitely beyond our highest prayers, desires, thoughts, or hopes'' (Eph. 3:20).

It is God who does the work in us, and it makes sense that the more we trust in Him and the less we depend on ourselves, the more He is able to do.

So what exactly *is* the baptism in the Holy Spirit?

Jesus often referred to the Holy Spirit as the Spirit of Truth. ''When the Holy Spirit, who is truth, comes, he shall guide you into all truth'' (John 16:13).

The Holy Spirit of Truth lives in *all* believers and guides them, but to be baptized in the Spirit of Truth means a great deal more. The word we translate as ''baptize'' in our English Bible actually means to immerse or saturate, and in Greek the same word is used to describe ''waterlogged.''

So to ask Jesus to baptize us in the Holy Spirit means that we surrender ourselves to be saturated — waterlogged with His Truth.

Jesus prayed for us to His Father. ''Sanctify them — purify, consecrate, separate them for Yourself, make them holy — by the Truth'' (John 17:17 *Amplified Bible*).

The baptism in the Holy Spirit is a cleansing, purging, stripping experience; it is total exposure to the searchlight of God's Truth into every little corner of our lives. The baptism is designed to flush out and empty us of our self-reliance, our pride, our little shady areas of deception, and the excuses we've been holding onto — all the things that block our faith and the inflow of God's power and presence in our lives.

The baptism in or with the Holy Spirit serves a twofold purpose: the purging and preparing of the vessel to *contain* God's power and then the *filling* with the power. The two events occur simultaneously, because when the Holy Spirit of Truth begins to saturate our beings, it exposes and drives out all the junk and debris we've let pile up inside us.

Jesus said, ''But you shall receive power — ability, efficiency and might — *when* the Holy Spirit has come upon you'' (Acts 1:8 *Amplified Bible*).

He didn't mean that the power would belong to us, but it would fill us, and operate through us. We are the containers, the vessels, the channels. However hard we try, we can't become the contents. We are like glasses containing living water. The water can quench men's thirst, but an empty glass can't satisfy anyone.

Paul wrote, "But this precious treasure — this light and power that now shine within us — is held in a perishable container, that is, in our weak bodies. Everyone can see that the glorious power within must be from God and is not our own" (II Cor. 4:7).

To say that we don't need the baptism in the Holy Spirit is the same as to say that we don't need to be cleansed, immersed in, and saturated by God's Truth, nor do we need the fullness of His power operating in and through us.

Jesus told His followers, "You men who are fathers — if your boy asks for bread, do you give him a stone? If he asks for fish, do you give him a snake? If he asks for an egg, do you give him a scorpion? [Of course not!] And if even sinful persons like yourselves give children what they need, don't you realize that your heavenly Father will do at least as much, and give the Holy Spirit to those who ask for Him?" (Luke 11:11-13).

So we can ask Jesus to baptize us in the Holy Spirit and *know* that He does it.

Every week I get letters from people who say they've pleaded with God to baptize them in the Holy Spirit, but nothing has happened. What's wrong? The trouble is they are looking at their own feelings instead of at God's fact. The stumbling block is *always* feelings.

The baptism in the Holy Spirit, like every one of God's gifts, must be received in *faith*. That means you may not *feel* anything when it happens. Faith is an act of our will, not a response to feelings.

Now some people experience dramatic physical sensations when they are first baptized in the Holy Spirit, just as some people have a dramatic, emotional encounter with Jesus Christ when they first receive Him as their Savior. But we don't get saved by feeling, and we don't get baptized in the Holy Spirit by feeling either. Whatever outward sensations you may or may not feel when you're baptized in the Holy Spirit, the sensations are *not* the baptism. The baptism is an *inner* transformation.

As a *result* of this inner transformation, we are told in the Bible, there will be plenty of evidence to follow. Increased power

49

and authority in witnessing for Christ, the operation of the gifts of the Holy Spirit through us, the increasing fruit of the Spirit — the love, joy, peace. All these things we'll experience with our senses, but these evidences follow our acceptance of God's fact; we cannot measure them by our feelings.

We must decide to accept God's Word on faith and deliberately turn from paying attention to our feelings. If we don't, we will never be able to exercise our faith.

Tell God that you *will* take His Word for it. You *will* to believe Jesus baptizes you when you ask Him to. *Stand* firm in your trust and *know* it has happened.

One young man wrote me:

"I am planning to enter seminary next fall, but my Christian life lacks power. I meet with a group of Christians who've experienced the baptism in the Holy Spirit. They pray and speak in tongues, and there are healings and miracles happening. I'm convinced this is all valid according to the scriptures, and I've prayed to receive it, but for some reason or other it hasn't happened to me. I know that the gifts of the Holy Spirit aren't given for our personal enjoyment, but for the work God would have us do. Still, God hasn't trusted me with this experience. What is lacking? I wonder. I believe in the Lord Jesus Christ as my Savior and want to serve Him with all my heart. I've told Him so, many times. I've confessed my sins, both in church and in private prayer, and I know I'm forgiven and cleansed. I want to serve Christ, and I need the baptism in the Holy Spirit to do so effectively. Why then, hasn't it happened? Have I done something wrong so that God doesn't hear my prayer?

"Yesterday I knelt in our prayer meeting and asked that I be allowed to receive the baptism in the Holy Spirit. Several placed their hands on me and prayed that I might receive. But I didn't feel a thing...Please pray for me."

It doesn't matter where you are or what words you use in asking for the baptism in the Holy Spirit. It doesn't matter if you're alone or if someone else prays for you with the laying on of hands. The baptism in the Holy Spirit is a personal matter between you and the Baptizer, Jesus Christ.

You need ask only once, then thank God that He has heard

your request and granted it. If you prayed last week and nothing seemed to happen,, then you are letting your senses fool you. Jesus did His part; now it is up to you to believe it is done.

You may not feel anything, but there is one tangible consequence you can claim right away and experience the result. The gift of tongues was recorded as a consequence of the baptism in the Holy Spirit in the Book of Acts. It was the *first* operation of a spiritual gift in the newly baptized believers.

When I asked Jesus to baptize me with the Holy Spirit, I didn't feel a thing. A lady laid hands on me and prayed for me in tongues, but I felt no physical sensation then, and thought that nothing had happened. The lady told me to accept the baptism on faith, not to depend on my feelings, and to thank God that it was already done. I did it, but felt a little ridiculous. Then the lady told me I could speak with tongues if I just opened my mouth and let the language pour out. I hesitated and thought that now I was really making a fool of myself. But I knew that the Bible said speaking in tongues *was* a gift of the Holy Spirit, and since I now was filled with the Holy Spirit — whether I could feel it or not — I could expect the Holy Spirit to operate in me and through me. I did notice some strange "words" forming in my mind, and I opened my mouth and said them out loud. They sounded silly, and my instant reaction was to think, *You're faking it Merlin; you're just making up a bunch of gibberish.* Then I realized that speaking *on faith* meant I couldn't rely on my own senses to measure the results. I decided to accept God's word for it and not pay attention to what *I* thought.

I had still *felt* nothing, but I had made up my mind to *believe.* The first evidence I could register with my feelings was an overwhelming awareness that Jesus Christ was my Savior and Lord. I knew from the Word of God that the Holy Spirit had been sent to witness about Jesus, and I was suddenly convinced more than ever before of Who Jesus was and what He meant to me. The second evidence I felt was a strong sense of love for people. That, too, was foretold in God's Word. Love is a fruit of the Holy Spirit.

Since then I've experienced the operation of some of the other gifts of the Holy Spirit in and through me as well. I haven't been given the ability to heal or to perform miracles or to prophesy. I only *believe* that God operates through me in the power of the Holy Spirit when I step out on faith, expecting Him to do so.

When someone is healed after I have laid hands on him and prayed, it is not because I've become extraspiritual. I'm just the channel. When I pray, I sometimes *feel* the presence of God's healing power and sometimes I feel absolutely nothing.

The results never depend on our feelings, only on our faith, that is, our deliberate choice to believe that God is at work.

When you open your mouth and begin to speak in tongues on faith, you will probably be tempted to think just as I did, that you are faking it and making up the words: Don't let that thought fool you into giving up the practice.

If you have sincerely committed yourself and your tongue to God, asking that the Holy Spirit will give you the words to pray, then you can trust that He is doing just that, whether the words sound like made-up nonsense to your ears or not. It isn't really the words that matter anyway, but the fact that the Holy Spirit is praying through us directly to God.

But why then pray at all — in tongues or in English — if God knows what we need before we even ask Him?

We pray, because this is God's plan for His children, and His explicit command to us as well.

"Pray without ceasing" (I Thess. 5:17 KJV).

It is very important that we take time to pray in tongues daily. Just think for a moment what we're actually doing. The Holy Spirit of Truth is speaking through us.

Jesus promised that "rivers of living water shall flow from the inmost being of anyone who believes in me" (John 7:38).

He was speaking of the rivers of truth flowing from our innermost being when we have been immersed in and saturated by the Holy Spirit of Truth.

We often think only of the truth that will flow out to others, but think now what the truth first must do in us. Truth is the power that sets our bound-up spirits free. It exposes every hidden lie, every guilt and fear, all the dark areas of our past lurking in the back of our memories, way back in our subconscious soul. We couldn't even begin to talk to God about those things *with our understanding*. And this is one of the reasons *God devised* this new dimension in prayer.

But when we speak in tongues, we communicate directly from our spirit to God. The Holy Spirit prays *for* us, and we bypass the control-center of our own critical understanding. We speak words we don't understand, but the Holy Spirit of Truth searches out the deep areas of our beings. That's what gives speaking in tongues such a great healing power in our own lives. Later we'll discover that when we pray in tongues for others, we pray directly for needs that we don't know anything about with our understanding, and often the people we pray for have no idea what the root of their problem is either.

A housewife who had suffered with serious mental and emotional problems since her early teens accepted Christ as her Savior. But she did not experience a release from the deep tensions that plagued her. She studied what the Bible had to say about the baptism in the Holy Spirit and became convinced God wanted her to experience it.

One day she knelt in her living room and prayed, "I surrender all of me to you, Jesus. Cleanse me of everything that isn't of you, and baptize me in your Holy Spirit. I thank you, and I believe it has been done."

She felt no sensation of any kind and got up from her knees to continue with her housework, but over the next three weeks, something unusual seemed to be going on inside her. She wept almost continuously, and it was as if she was reliving again the early years of her unhappy childhood. Long-forgotten incidents came back to her memory, things others had done to leave scars of hurt and fear, and things she had done to hurt others. With each memory came a surge of repentant tears, and she found herself asking God to forgive her and those who had hurt her and to heal the memories with His love.

She could think of only one explanation for all her tears, the verse in her Bible which read, "And in the same way — by our faith — the Holy Spirit helps us with our daily problems and in our praying. For we don't even know what we should pray for, nor how to pray as we should; but the Holy Spirit prays for us with such feeling and pleads in our behalf with unspeakable yearnings and groanings too deep for utterance" (Rom. 8:26 *Living Bible* and *Amplified Bible*).

In between the crying sessions, she felt increasingly at ease. Then came one evening at the end of the third week when she cried and cried as if her heart was breaking.

"I felt as if the convulsions of tears were coming from the very pit of my being," she recalled. "Then suddenly it eased off, as if a storm had gone away, leaving behind a beautiful calm. I rested in that peace when suddenly I became aware of a light flowing gently over me from above. It could be felt more than seen, and I knew it was the love of God, surrounding me, holding me..."

Many of her tensions were gone — but not all. Over the next few days she felt lighter at heart than ever before, and she sang to herself as she did her housework or drove errands to town. Over and over she sang a simple chorus she had taught her children. "Oh how I love Jesus, oh, how I love Jesus..." The song had suddenly taken on a new and happier meaning.

One afternoon she was driving downtown and realized that she was putting make-believe words to the tune she was singing.

"I didn't know what was happening," she said later. "I hadn't really paid much attention to what the Bible had to say about speaking in tongues, but there I was singing in a new language and I suddenly realized it wasn't 'make-believe,' but it had something to do with being baptized in the Holy Spirit."

She continued singing in tongues every day, and as the weeks and months passed, her old tensions and emotional distress vanished.

"The psychiatrist had told me that I would just have to accept myself as an emotional cripple," she said, "but praise God, He healed me. I sang my way to wholeness — in tongues!"

If you have prayed to be baptized in the Holy Spirit, you can take God's Word for it, it is done. You may open your mouth right now and speak whatever words or sounds happen to come to your mind, trusting that it is the Holy Spirit who is placing them in your mind.

God will not force you to speak in tongues. With the baptism in the Holy Spirit, He has given you the ability to speak in tongues, but only if you choose to do so. You use your mouth, your tongue, and your vocal chords, and you can begin speaking and stop speaking at will. If you feel no emotion or sensation of any kind, praise God *for* your lack of feeling. One day you *will* feel, but in the meantime He is giving you a wonderful opportunity to grow in faith.

In your Bible, read everything Jesus had to say about the Holy Spirit; read the Book of Acts and the letters to the young churches concerning the Holy Spirit, the gifts of the Spirit, and the fruit of the Spirit. All that applies to you now.

Expect these things to happen in your own life. Tell God you are willing to be used as a channel for His love to others, and be ready to step out on faith when God provides the opportunities.

Praise God in all circumstances, whether they seem good or bad to you; trust that God is using them to unfold His wonderful plan for your life.

4

Count It All Joy!

"Dear brothers, is your life full of difficulties and temptations? Then be happy, for when the way is rough, your patience has a chance to grow. So let it grow, and don't try to squirm out of your problems. For when your patience is finally in full bloom, then you will be ready for anything, strong in character, full and complete" (James 1:2-4).

God has a very special plan for your life. It began long ago when He first created you. He formed you lovingly, carefully, exactly to His specifications, every detail just as He wanted it — your looks, your abilities, your place of birth, the family you were to be born into (or the lack of it!). Nothing about you or your life has been accidental up to this point. In love he reached out and drew you to Himself through circumstances He had arranged just for that purpose. You were given a new birth, new life through His Holy Spirit when you accepted His Son, Jesus Christ, as your Savior, and were baptized, saturated with the Holy Spirit. And now God's plan is to make you full and complete!

"For because of our faith, he has brought us into this place of highest privilege where we now stand, and we confidently and joyfully look forward to *actually becoming* all that God has had in mind for us to be" (Rom. 5:2).

God wants us to *become* something.

Why of course, we all know that! God wants us to become more loving, more kind, more patient, have more faith, peace, gentleness, kindness, humility, and self-discipline, so that we can be His witnesses wherever we are! Isn't that true?

Sure it is, but most of us think that means we have to embark on a rigorous program of self-improvement, trying to make ourselves more loving, kind, patient, humble, gentle, and disciplined. And the harder we try, the more frustrated we become.

God has to do the changing. He wants us to commit ourselves to Him and trust that He will transform us.

"With eyes wide open to the mercies of God, I beg you, my brothers, as an act of intelligent worship, to give him your bodies, as a living sacrifice, consecrated to him, and acceptable by him. Don't let the world around you squeeze you into its own mold, but let God remold your minds from within, so that you may prove in practice that the plan of God for you is good, meets all His demands and moves toward the goal of true maturity" (Rom. 12:1-2 Phillips).

How does God bring about the changes in us? *How* does He break with the old habit-patterns of thought and action we've lived with for years — characteristics we've called "personality-traits," or "personal likes and dislikes," or "preferences," or "strong opinions," that on closer examination, under the scrutiny of God's Holy Spirit of Truth, are seen to be part of the self-centered, defensive, selfish behavior that for years had separated us from the love of God and the love of others.

What methods does God use to change us?

"At present you are temporarily harassed by all kinds of trials and temptations. This is no accident — it happens to prove your faith, which is infinitely more valuable than gold... [which] must be purified by fire. This proving of your faith is planned to result in praise and honor and glory in the day when Jesus Christ reveals Himself" (I Pet. 1:6-7 Phillips).

So that is how our faith grows! And we read earlier how patience, endurance, and steadfastness grow when our life is full of difficulties, temptations, and problems.

I've heard some people say, "If that's the only way to get more patience and faith, I think I'd just as soon live with a little less of it!"

If that's the way you think, it is because you don't really trust

58

God. Deep down you have your doubts about His plan and His love for you.

When God showed His prophet Jeremiah that he would have to go with the Jews into Babylonian captivity for a lifetime, God also said, "For I know the plans I have for you, says the Lord. They are plans for good and not for evil, to give you a future and a hope" (Jer. 29:11).

The years of suffering in Babylon were part of God's plan for Jeremiah and the Jews. It was a good plan, the best plan, designed to give them a future and a hope.

God's plan for you and for me is a good plan. Can you take His Word for that?

Why can't our faith grow in pleasant, easy circumstances? It does, as we come to trust and rely more and more on God's promises. But the purifying, the testing of our faith, has to come through circumstances that are a challenge to our determination to believe, trust, rely on God's word, *in spite of* what our senses tell us. For so long we've trusted our senses, our emotions, and our intellect to dictate our beliefs. We must be broken of that habit in order to exercise faith. Faith, remember, means a deliberate determination to believe something we can't see or feel the evidence of.

So if God tells us He's working everything out for our good, and we see everything go wrong, our faith grows when we stand on God's Word and thank Him for everything that happens.

How do you think Abraham's faith grew?

Would you have faith to walk up on a mountain with your only son, prepared to sacrifice him on the altar at God's command, and still believe that God was going to bless and multiply your descendants through that same son?

If you had been a friend of Abraham's, could you have watched his crazy venture in faith and praised God, believing that even if Abraham was making a mistake, God would still work it out for good?

God alone can remake us, remold us from within. Our part is to follow Paul's advice to the Romans; to submit ourselves fully to Him, believe that He has taken over, and then accept eagerly and joyfully with thanksgiving and praise all the circumstances God uses to bring about his transformation of our lives.

59

There is the classic story of the pastor who prayed for more patience, and discovered the next day that his longtime efficient secretary had become ill. In her place was a volunteer who turned out to be the slowest office-worker the pastor had ever seen. He fussed and fumed in secret for a while, until he finally realized that the new secretary was an answer to his prayer. How else could he learn more patience? He began to thank and praise God for His choice of secretary and she soon improved remarkably.

Faith and patience are essential characteristics of a Christian life and witness; yet there is another quality we must have or else we've missed the point of Good News.

"Let love be your greatest aim," Paul wrote to the Corinthians (I Cor. 14:1).

"Your strong love for each other will prove to the world that you are my disciples," said Jesus (John 13:25).

"This is My commandment, that you love one another [just] as I have loved you...that your joy...may be full," Jesus said (John 15:12, 11 *Amplified Bible*).

Love...love...love...As Christians we talk a great deal about it. *God is love, Jesus loves you, I love you.* But we fall woefully short of really loving one another.

Jesus said, "I *demand* that you love each other as much as I love you" (John 15:12).

Love means more to us than anything else in the world. We were created to love God and to love one another. When we don't love, fearful things happen in us. We become hurt, resentful, afraid of each other, hateful, and guilt-ridden.

The wounds of our emotions, our fears and frustrations, our defense mechanisms, our destructive ways — all have come about for lack of love.

Educators, psychologists, sociologists, and all kinds of experts have told us what a difference love makes in the development of human beings.

A love that accepts, approves of, believes in others, is patient, kind, never selfish or envious, never proud or seeking its own reward or way, not touchy or irritable, doesn't hold grudges, and doesn't pay attention when it must suffer wrong. A love that is loyal, that believes the best and expects the best, is never glad when someone suffers wrong, but always happy when truth wins out. Such a love endures without weakening in all circumstances.

This is the kind of love God has for us, and the kind of love He commands that we have for each other. This is the kind of love that heals the wounds of old hurts, casts out old fears, melts away resentments and old grudges. This is the kind of love that makes us whole and able to love in return without fear of being rejected or hurt.

This is the love the Greeks called *agape*, a deliberate, reasoning, intentional, spiritual devotion. This is the love that is a fruit of the Holy Spirit, and when it is fully grown, it is the light that draws others to its source — God's love for us in Christ Jesus.

Every one of the gifts and manifestations of the Holy Spirit is given specifically to show God's love and concern for our every need. God heals because He loves; He performs miracles because He loves. God *is* love, and His power in us and through us is love — a supernatural, divine, intensely personal love for each individual in His creation.

His message to the world is one of love, and we are to be His messengers, the channels for His love. In order to accomplish this, His plan is to make *us* loving too.

But if love can only come to us from God, if it is a fruit of the Holy Spirit, how can Jesus command us to love? Mustn't we wait till He makes us more loving? Again we are faced with a promise in God's word that we must accept on faith.

Love is a fruit of the Spirit, and God's word says that the Holy Spirit dwells in us, therefore we can expect love to be present in our life. We have been given the ability to love, but we must step out on faith and choose to practice it.

Remember, *agape* is a deliberate, intentional love. We are told to love each other, even if we don't *feel* loving.

When we step out on faith, choosing to act on God's word, then what happens? We know that our step of faith releases God's supernatural power of love, and this power begins to transform us, *making* us more loving, while the power also flows through us to the person we've deliberately *willed* to love.

How does that actually work in practice?

I had prayed for God to make me more loving, and had come to think of myself as a not too unloving sort of person. In fact as I traveled and ministered to thousands of people all of whom seemed to be blessed, I rejoiced that I was able to feel more love for others all the time.

Then one day I was faced with an individual so miserable and repulsive that I cringed at the sight and realized to my horror that I felt no love for this creature, but only wished that she would disappear as soon as possible.

She was a girl who had been brought to my office with her soldier boyfriend. Her face was caked with old makeup and dirt, her hair hung like strands of wire, and her clothes were filthy and torn. Her legs were scarred and smeared with dirt, and the odor from her body filled the room. The expression on her face was sullen and hateful, and her eyes were swollen from crying.

This poor creature had come to Fort Benning to tell the soldier that she was expecting his baby. The boy admitted that he was responsible for her condition, but had flatly refused to marry her. The girl had flown into a rage and threatened to kill him and then herself. She had already had another baby out of wedlock, and this time she was determined to either get married or die.

I looked at her and thought I had never seen anyone so unlovable, so desperate, so frightened, and so lonely. Yet, the very thought of praying for her was offensive to me. I didn't want to touch her.

"Lord," I cried inwardly, "why did you bring her to me?"

"She's one of my children," came the answer. "She is lost and in need of my love and healing. I brought her here for you to love her and tell her of my love."

The painful realization hit me suddenly. I had boasted to myself of being able to love, yet now I cringed at the sight of one who desperately needed to be loved.

"O, Lord," I cried inside, "forgive me, and thank you for showing me just how shallow and selfish my love is. Take my unlovingness and fill me with your love for her."

The girl was sobbing and her eyes looked dull behind the swollen lids smeared with mascara.

"Please, Sir," she said, "do something!"

"Do you believe in God?"

She nodded and whispered, "Yes, I do."

"Do you believe He can help you?"

She hesitated, then spoke slowly. "I know He *can* help me, but I don't think He'd want to. I used to be a Christian, but look at me now. Even if He wanted to help me, what could He do to get me out of this mess?"

"God *can* help you, and He *wants* to," I said with an assurance I didn't yet feel.

She shook her head and her shoulders sagged in utter hopelessness.

"Please," I said, "Try to understand that God loves you. He will fill you with His joy and peace and meet your every need before you leave my office today."

The girl stared, openmouthed, and the soldier looked as if he thought I was going to force him to marry the girl.

"God has brought you here today," I continued. "He has permitted all the troubles in your life just so that you could understand how much He loves you. He has a wonderful plan for your life, and if you begin to trust Him and thank Him for everything that has happened to you, you will discover that God is helping you right now."

"Thank Him for this?" Her eyes blazed in sudden anger again. "All I want is for this man to marry me so my child will have a name."

"Look here." I showed her the underlined verse in my open Bible. "In every thing give thanks, for this is the will of God in Christ Jesus concerning you" (I Thess. 5:18 KJV). I flipped the pages to Rom. 8:28 (KJV). "All things work together for good to them that love God."

Her eyes stared in blank mistrust, and I suddenly realized how futile it was to speak to this wounded creature about God's love or any kind of love. She didn't know the meaning of the word. Only God could light the spark of understanding in her mind.

"May I pray for you?"

She nodded dully. "Sure, why not?"

I moved to place my hand on her head, and as I looked down I saw just how dirty and in need of a scrubbing she was. The twinge of revulsion made me shudder.

"Oh, Lord," I whispered, "how endless your love is for us — so much greater than the little love we are capable of on our own. Please, God, let your love touch her now, and teach me to love her."

Then I placed my hand firmly on her head and began to pray out loud.

"God, I know it is your will that we praise you in everything. Nothing in this world can happen without your will and permission. This dear child of yours has been hurt. She is sick, bruised, forsaken, and unloved by man, but I know you love her. Thank you for all that has brought her to this day in her life. Help her, Lord. I believe you are helping her to see your love and to praise you right now. . . ."

I felt the girl begin to tremble under my hand. God was touching her with His love.

"Can you thank God for everything now?"

"Oh, yes," she burst out. "I thank you, God. I really do thank you for everything."

I continued to pray. "God, I believe you are healing this broken spirit. You are putting new life into her; you are giving her joy in the place of sorrow, victory in the place of defeat."

When I stepped back, her face shone with tears.

"What happened?" she exclaimed. "I feel so different! I'm not all churned up inside anymore; it's so quiet in me. I've never felt like this before. I'm happy; I really am!" Her eyes were wide with surprise. "What did it?"

"God has done it because we believed Him and praised Him," I said, suddenly realizing that something equally miraculous had happened in me. I stared at the girl, and she looked like a different person. I wanted to put my arms around her. She seemed so beautiful, so clean, so holy!

"Thank you, Lord." I felt my spirit soaring upward. "I *love* that girl. Thank you for changing *me,* Lord."

I could never have made myself more loving by trying to change my attitude toward the girl. God had to do the changing. My part was to admit and confess my own lack of love, then submit in faith to God's transforming power in willingness to love.

The harder we try to change ourselves, the more frustrated

we become, and the more guilty we feel about our own shortcomings.

God brings certain people into our lives just to show us how incapable we are of loving others in our own strength. He doesn't do it to make us feel bad; He does it to give us an opportunity to experience His transforming love in our life and in the lives of the people He has called us to love.

Do you thank Him for the people in your life who are difficult to love? Do you have a cranky neighbor? A difficult boss? Praise God for them, because He loves you and wants to make your joy full by making it possible for you to love them. He loves them too, and wants to use you as a channel for His love to them.

I think perhaps the most wonderful and most challenging opportunities to love come in our own homes, right where we live. Does your husband or wife have certain qualities that rub you the wrong way? Are your parents difficult to live with? Your children rebellious?

Love one another, Jesus said. Accept one another; thank God for one another.

It isn't easy to thank God for an alcoholic husband or for an indifferent, rebellious child. It isn't easy to love someone who says he doesn't want our love.

It isn't easy to admit that beam in our eye, the self-righteousness, the self-pity, the role we've played as a long-suffering martyr. Can we thank God for bringing the people into our lives to show us the beam in our eye?

Can we thank God for them, just as they are, and especially for the things that make them hard to love? Can we confess our inability to love them *for* their irritating habits? Can we tell God we *want* to love them and then submit ourselves to Him to be remolded, remade, so that we can love them perfectly, according to His will and plan for us?

Then we can confidently expect God to work a miracle in us. It may happen instantaneously; we *feel* a wonderful spark of love, and of course we rejoice and praise the Lord for that. But watch out and don't become dependent on feelings. That first spark may die down, and we may sit around waiting for a second touch without doing anything in the meantime.

To love, deliberately and intentionally as Christ loves us, always requires the setting of our will. Whether we *feel* any love to begin with or not doesn't change the fact that we *do* love. God will show us practical and specific ways to communicate that love to the person He has placed in our life, and soon we will experience and sense a deeper love than any we've ever felt before. Our love will be stable and consistent, because it flows from a source beyond our own limited resources. It is God's love filling us to overflowing, spilling over to others through us. This is what it means to be rooted in God's love; and in that fertile soil, our own ability to love will grow and grow.

That is how the Holy Spirit bears fruit in our lives.

A Christian woman had been married to an alcoholic for many years until finally he got into trouble with the law and ended up in prison. The wife had struggled to raise their children on the meager welfare allowance they received from the state. Faithfully she had brought them to church and enjoyed the sympathy and respect of her community.

"Poor Edna," her friends would say. "She's raised those kids alone, never missed a Sunday in church, and never a word of complaint. While that good-for-nothing husband of hers never has been able to hold down a job, lying drunk most of the time to the disgrace and shame of his fine family..."

While her husband was in prison, Edna felt justified in getting a divorce. Now at last, she would be free to raise her children in a better environment.

One day a friend brought her a copy of *Prison to Praise*.

It seemed an almost impossible task to thank God for all the years of misery she had suffered, but she read how praise had changed the lives of others, and she decided to try it.

"Thank you for Al and his drinking," she prayed. "Thank you for the years of poverty and fear and loneliness."

Soon she heard that her former husband had been released from prison and had gone back to his old drinking habits. Still she continued to thank God for her circumstances.

Slowly she became aware of some things in her own life that she had never seen before. As she continued to thank God for her ex-husband, asking God to help her love him and accept him just as he was, she began to realize that for years she'd been guilty of something far more serious than drinking.

She'd been looking at the mote in her husband's eye and been totally unaware of the beam in her own. She had judged him for his drinking, feeling self-righteous and worthier than he was, and at the same time she'd lived each day steeped in self-pity, depression, and joyless martyrdom.

"Oh, Lord," she finally cried out one day, "I see that my sin has been so much graver than Al's. You gave us the commandment to love one another and to rejoice in our trials, and I didn't love or find any joy. Forgive me, Lord, and thank you for putting Al in my life so I could see myself. Now make it up to him. Heal the hurts he's suffered, and touch him with your love."

From that day on, Edna found it easy to rejoice in her circumstances. She *knew* God had brought them about as a part of His plan to fill her life with love and joy. As she continued to praise Him, all the old feelings of self-pity and depression rolled away; each day became a new, joyous experience, and she was aware of the presence of Jesus Christ in a new, exciting way.

Before long her former husband stumbled into a church service, accepted Christ as his Savior, and was completely healed of the alcoholism which had held him bound for fifteen years. Edna and Al remarried, and Al enrolled in college to start a brand-new life of serving God.

A difficult relationship or a trying set of circumstances may be God's loving way of providing us with an opportunity to grow, to exercise our spiritual muscle or it may be His loving way of exposing a particular weakness or error in us.

Whatever the reason, we have grounds to rejoice. Any weakness, however well hidden, is like a crack in the foundation of a building.

"Therefore this iniquity and guilt shall be to you as a broken section of a high wall, bulging out and ready [at some distant day] to fall, whose crash will then come suddenly and swiftly, in an instant" (Isa. 30:13 *Amplified Bible*).

Sooner or later, a crack in the foundation will cause the entire building to fall down. The cracks we are aware of, we can do something about. We can confess all our known sins and weaknesses and be assured that once they are confessed, they are also forgiven, and God's love covers and heals the scars and the memories. But what about the hidden cracks, the hidden sins that come to the surface only as a vague sense of restlessness, insecurity, confusion, resentment, or any number of such symptoms we all know from experience?

The particular iniquity Isaiah was referring to in the verse above was the Israelites' repeated refusal to act on God's Word; instead, they sought the counsel of their own seers and human advisers. They preferred to rely on themselves instead of on God.

Self-reliance and self-assurance are always serious cracks in our foundation. If God brings us into circumstances that reveal an area of life where we've been relying on ourselves, shouldn't we thank Him for our helplessness and rejoice in the power He can give us?

A young man in officer's training at Fort Benning, Georgia, found himself in circumstances he couldn't cope with.

"I need help, or I'll go out of my mind," he told me.

He had always been sure he could face every circumstance in life with success. His self-assurance bordered on cockiness. But since coming to officer candidate school, he had found himself unable to function as before, and his self-image and entire outlook on life was shattered.

The rigorous training for officer candidates is designed not only to teach the young men their duties as army officers, but is also meant to expose any weakness in the candidate that might endanger the lives of his men in combat. A certain stress is deliberately put on the candidates to test what "stuff" they are made of; if any are going to crack under pressure, it is better to find out before they are put in charge of troops.

The instructors had sensed that this particular candidate was unsure of himself under the mask of self-sufficiency he wore. The pressure had been put on. From early morning until late at night he was under surveillance. Every move he made was criticized.

"Can't you move faster, candidate?"

"Are you too dumb to follow instructions?"

"Do you always eat like a pig?"

"Don't you have any backbone?"

"Do you want your mother to help you?"

"Run around the building once more, candidate — maybe you'll learn to pick up your feet!"

The confidence the candidate had felt in himself was rapidly diminishing. Humiliated and helpless, he was at his wit's end, ready to desert the army and leave the country if necessary to get away from his persecutors.

As we talked, he told me that he'd never really believed in God, and the Bible had never made much sense to him. But if there was a God who could help him, he wanted to believe.

I shared with him what the Bible had to say about his circumstances, that God had a perfect plan for his life, that the trials he was going through were part of that plan, and that God would relieve all the tension and stress if he would only turn over the reins of his life to Him and thank Him for everything.

The candidate looked drawn; his face and eyes showed the strain and lack of sleep.

"I've never been in this kind of spot before." He shook his head. "I'm at the end of my rope, and now you're telling me that God placed me in this predicament?"

"Let's say that God allowed it to happen," I said. I'm sure He would rather have had you turn to Him and accept His provisions for your life without having to go through all this suffering. But since you kept insisting you could handle your life without help, God chose the most direct, most loving way to show you that you needed Him."

I turned to Paul's second letter to the Corinthians and read, "We should like you, our brothers, to know something of what we went through in Asia. At that time we were completely overwhelmed; the burden was more than we could bear; in fact we told ourselves that this was the end. Yet we believe now that we had this experience of coming to the end of our tether that we might learn to trust, not in ourselves, but in God" (II Cor. 1:8-9 Phillips).

The candidate looked thoughtful, and agreed to let me pray for him, although he wasn't at all sure it would do any good.

I placed my hand on his head and began to praise God for the situation, asking God to give the young candidate a new understanding of His love and concern for every detail of his life. As I prayed, he began to tremble; then tears began to flow. After a while he began to laugh out loud.

"Praise you, God," he cried. "Thank you, God; I see you care; I believe you love me."

He turned to me, his face beaming.

"God really did bring me to officer candidate school, didn't He?" he said. "He knew this is where I'd find the answer. I feel like a new person."

And indeed he was. He accepted Christ as his Savior and went on to complete OCS with excellent standing.

The crisis point in his life had revealed a serious crack in his foundation. When he could acknowledge and thank God for His hand in the circumstances, the crack was healed.

Circumstances that rip out the walls of our own self-sufficiency are God's blessings in disguise. We can truly thank God for them and praise Him for every blow that removes more of the illusion that we have the ability to handle our own situation. The more we praise Him, the easier the transition will be. Our joy will increase, and the pain will hardly be noticeable. We'll also discover that the more trying the circumstances, the more we will realize the real strength and power of Christ dwelling and growing in us.

Each challenge, each trial or opportunity for growth makes us better equipped to be channels for His love and power.

A young girl was faced with a series of tragedies. Her mother and two of her brothers died. Her father remarried, divorced, and remarried again. The girl was failing in college, and drinking heavily. Then she heard about Jesus and accepted Him as her Savior. For a time she was filled with joy, and as she shared her story, others came to know Jesus Christ. Her life was going smoothly, and she thought all the hard times were over.

Then the troubles began to pile up. She was in two automobile accidents and was injured in both of them. Next, a tumor appeared on her neck and had to be removed by a painful operation. One day she drank a coke and became seriously ill — the coke had been spiked with drugs. On her way to school she was badly frightened by an attacker with a knife; another day a man came after her with a gun. Prowlers came to her house at night; one of them broke in and raped her. At last she was fired from her part-time job because her boss was certain that she must be doing something wrong to get herself into all that trouble.

Through it all the girl struggled to hold onto her faith. The hardest burden to bear was the mistrust and suspicion of the church people she knew.

Then someone placed a copy of *Prison to Praise* in her hand. She read it and caught new hope. Perhaps God had a reason for permitting all the trouble she was going through. She began thanking Him for each calamity that had come into her life, and as she did, joy replaced the fear that had been gripping her.

"I suddenly realized that God is all I have," she told me. "Other people may have security. I have only Him, and everything that has happened has made me see this more clearly."

This young lady now goes about with a new, radiant power to witness for her Savior. She has a deepened understanding and compassion for others who suffer as she did.

She had learned to trust that all the circumstances of her life were controlled by God's loving hand, and she could look at every new trial and say, "I know that God allowed it, so it must be for my good."

Another young woman lost her husband suddenly. They had no children, and she felt indescribably lonely. When she went to seek comfort and sympathy from her own family, they refused to speak to her, and behaved as if she didn't exist.

She couldn't understand this total rejection. Her family had never treated her like this before, and the anguish of being alone and unwanted was more than she could bear. Her body was in pain, she was unable to sleep, and she began to lose weight rapidly.

Day and night she cried alone in her house, until she began

to lose track of time. She realized that her mind was slipping.

In despair she cried out, "God, are you there? Do you care about me?" She heard no answer and found no relief.

Then one day she saw *Prison to Praise* in a local bookstore. She read on the back cover that the author was an army chaplain and put the book back on the counter. Her husband had been in the army when he died, and she was afraid of a fresh flood of memories. She went home empty-handed, but the title of the little book stayed in her mind all day, and one thought persisted: *Read it! Read it!*

She'd never felt such an urge to read anything before, and puzzled by the sense of urgency, she went back to the bookstore and purchased the little volume.

At home she began to read, and soon her tears started flowing. At times she cried so hard she couldn't see to read, and at one point she realized that she had sunk to her knees on the floor and was still reading on.

She was certain that God was speaking directly to her through the book, yet the message was an incredible one. Was He actually telling her to thank Him that her husband was dead? How could God be so cruel? Everything in her seemed to rebel against the idea. Yet, as she read on, her sobs became more quiet and a new peace entered her heart. Slowly her thoughts began to take a new turn.

God has been in everything to help me she thought. *He knew that with my husband alive I would never have sought for Him! If my brother and his family had comforted me with kindness and love, I would have clung to them. Now I'm completely alone, and I'm coming to God. Oh Jesus, I feel your presence! You are here with me, and I praise and thank God for everything that brought me to you!*

The peace she felt in her heart was greater than anything she'd ever known before, and for the next several days her life radiated with a joy that completely astounded her friends and neighbors who had watched with growing concern how she had been broken down by grief.

Soon her brother came to see her with a tearful confession:

"Can you forgive me?" he said. "There's been a terrible misunderstanding. Someone told us that you had told your neighbor that we had refused to give you any help when your husband was dying. We were foolish enough to believe them and felt so shocked and hurt that we didn't want to see you or talk to you." The brother was overcome with shame. "Today we heard that the people had been talking about another widow! And to think that we left you alone when you needed us the most."

"Don't be sorry," the young widow cheerfully replied. "Be thankful you made the mistake!"

"What do you mean, Sis?" The brother was not sure he'd heard right. "I let you down when you really needed me; do you want me to thank God for that?"

"That's right," she laughed, "If you hadn't turned your back on me, I wouldn't have discovered just how much God loves me!"

The story is not meant to give an excuse for listening to gossip or for ignoring people who need our love. But God wants us to understand that when we trust our lives to Him, we can be sure that no one can treat us unfairly unless God allows it for our good. We can thank Him for every unkind word or sneaky, underhanded back-stabbing that comes our way.

"God will bless you for this, if you endure the pain of undeserved suffering because you are conscious of his will. For what credit is there in enduring the beatings you deserve for having done wrong? But if you endure suffering even when you have done right, God will bless you for it" (I Pet. 2:19-20 *Good News for Modern Man*).

A rosebush must be pruned to bear perfect roses. Jesus said, "I am the true Vine, and my Father is the Gardener. He lops off every branch that doesn't produce. And he prunes those branches that bear fruit for even larger crops. He has already tended you by pruning you back for greater strength and usefulness by means of the commands I gave you" [John 15:1-3]

These are the commands Jesus gave:

" 'Love the Lord your God with *all* your heart, soul, and mind.' This is the first and greatest commandment. The second most important is similar: 'Love your neighbor as much as you love yourself' "(Matt. 22:38-39)

73

The love Jesus spoke of was a deliberate love, one that required the setting of our will to love, a love exercised in faith. Jesus described the nature of this love when He said, "Love one another as I have loved you" (John 15:12 RSV).

Anything in us that prevents us from obeying that command must be pruned away. We're only delaying and hindering His work in us if we balk and complain about the painful pruning circumstances. These things don't come to us by accident or by the quirk of some cruel fate, but because our loving Father is our loving Gardener. We can rejoice and thank Him, because He knows what is best for us.

A Christian officer candidate at Fort Benning received word that his wife had been committed to a mental hospital after a severe breakdown. The doctors gave a poor prognosis for her recovery and said that she would have to be in the hospital for an indefinite time.

When John came into my office, he could not speak at first. I watched his tall frame shake with sobs and tears coursed down his grief-lined face.

"Why, oh, why did it happen?" He fought to utter the words. "My wife and I have tried to live good Christian lives; why has God deserted us now?"

"God hasn't deserted you," I said. "He has a real purpose in letting your wife go to the hospital. Why don't we kneel and thank Him for it?"

John stared at me. "Sir, I'm a Lutheran, and I've never read anything like that in my Bible!"

"What about this verse?" I suggested. "Always give thanks for everything to our God and Father in the name of our Lord Jesus Christ" (Eph. 5:20).

John shook his head. "I know that verse," he said. "I've always thought it meant to thank God for good things. Thanking Him for bad things just doesn't seem scriptural. I always thought Paul was a little extreme when he wrote about taking pleasure in infirmities."

"I used to think so, too," I said. "But I've become convinced that Paul is right. When he speaks about rejoicing in infirmities, he obviously doesn't mean we are supposed to find pain pleasurable in itself. But Paul had come to see his suffering from a different perspective. He had learned that his pain served a

74

higher purpose and was part of God's loving plan for him."

John looked thoughtful. "I just don't know," he said slowly.

"Paul learned his lesson the hard way, too," I went on. "Remember his 'thorn in the flesh'?"

John nodded.

"Three times Paul asked to have it removed. He was obviously not rejoicing in his pain right then. And three times God answered him, 'No. But I am with you; that is all you need. My power shows up best in weak people.' Now I am glad to boast about how weak I am; I am glad to be a living demonstration of Christ's power, instead of showing off my own power and abilities" (II Cor. 12:9).

"Paul wasn't happy about his infirmities for their own sake," I continued. "He went on to tell the Corinthians, 'Since I know it is all *for Christ's good*, I am quite happy about "the thorn," and about insults and hardships, persecutions and difficulties; for when I am weak, then I am strong — the less I have, the more I depend on him' "(II Cor. 12:10).

John leafed thoughtfully through his Bible.

"I have faith that God is working in all things," he said at last. "But the rejoicing part is really hard for me."

"If we say we have faith but can't rejoice, doesn't that mean we haven't really committed ourselves to trusting that God is doing what is best?" I suggested.

John sat in silence, then he nodded with determination.

"I believe you're right," he said. "I want to try it."

We knelt together, and John's tall frame shook with sobs as he prayed, "God, I know you love my wife more than I do. I believe you're working out a wonderful plan for us."

The tears were flowing freely down his face, but his eyes shone with a new confidence.

"God is doing the right thing, Chaplain," he said. "I know it."

A few days later John applied for compassionate transfer so that he could be near his wife. The request was eventually granted, and he came to say good-bye.

"Wait till you hear the best part," he said excitedly. "God

has promised to heal my wife the moment I see her if I place my hands on her head and say, 'In Jesus' name be healed.' ''

I felt a twinge of doubt. What if John in his eagerness was jumping ahead of God? Then I, too, felt the assurance of the Holy Spirit, and placed my hand on John in a parting prayer.

"Father, you say that if two agree on earth concerning anything we ask for, you will do it for us [Matt. 18:19]. So now I agree with John that the moment he touches his wife, you will heal her."

Two weeks later John's letter came.

"It happened just like Jesus told us it would. My wife was standing in the psychiatrist's office when I first saw her. She looked terrible. The lines in her face and the fear in her eyes almost convinced me she was beyond help. But I knew I had to obey what God had told me, and so I walked over and put my hands on her. The moment I touched her something like a shock went through her, and I knew she was healed. I told the psychiatrist that she was healed, and he looked at me as if he thought *I* needed to be admitted. But they called me the next day, and the psychiatrist said, "I don't know how to account for it, but your wife seems to be well!" My wife is home now, happier than she's ever been before. She has been strengthened by the afflictions she suffered, and she now joins me in being thankful for all things. We've learned how much of Christ's healing power is released when we praise Him."

God's strength can replace our weakness when we come to Him, recognizing and admitting where we fall short. But so often we're ashamed to confess that we are weak, afraid that others and God will not accept us as we really are. This kind of thinking is rooted in the wrong idea that we must earn or deserve God's love.

A Christian general came to me one day and confessed that the strain of presenting a perfect image before his men was about to kill him. As we talked, I realized that this man, whom I'd often admired for his outward poise and confidence, had never been able to accept himself as he really was. He was obsessed by the fear that if he should ever relax, he would grievously disappoint his family and his men.

I suggested that it would ease his tension if he would thank

God for having created him exactly as he was.

"You mean, as I am today? Filled with fear and tension?" he asked, and I nodded.

"Do you think the God who created this universe and placed the stars in the heavens was any less careful when He created you? Nor has He been careless with the circumstances He has allowed into your life in order to show you how much He loves you."

The general came to several sessions in my office, and studied his Bible and read *Prison to Praise* with interest. Gradually he came to accept that God had a perfect plan for his life and that the continuous stress he'd felt was serving the purpose of bringing him to trust God.

He began to praise God for his anxieties, and a sense of peace slowly replaced the old habits of fear. For the first time in his life he was happy to be himself.

"As long as I thought that God couldn't love me with my weaknesses, I tried to hide them and consequently drifted farther and farther from the truth," he told me. "As soon as I was able to admit I was weak, and thank God for having made me that way, His love began to transform me, and He began to fill me with His peace."

David wrote:

"Let everyone bless God and sing his praises, for he holds our lives in his hand. And he holds our feet to the path. You have purified us with fire, O Lord, like silver in a crucible. You captured us in your net and laid great burdens on our backs. You sent troops to ride across our broken bodies. We went through fire and blood. But in the end you brought us into wealth and great abundance...For I cried to him for help, with praises ready on my tongue. He would not have listened if I had not confessed my sins. But He listened! He heard my prayer! He paid attention to it! Sing to the Lord, all the earth! Sing of His glorious name!" (Psa. 66:8-12, 17-19, 1-2).

David wanted oneness with God, and he knew that anything unclean in him would prevent God's love from filling him and flowing through him. Therefore David welcomed the purifying, the breaking and cleansing process God put him through. He rejoiced when the trials revealed the hidden sins of his own heart, sins he could confess and be healed of. God himself had shown David the way.

"I don't need your sacrifices of flesh and blood. What I want from you is your true thanks. . . *I want you to trust me in your times of trouble, so I can rescue you, and you can give me glory!* . . . Recite my laws no longer, and stop claiming my promises, for you have refused my discipline, disregarding my laws . . . This is the last chance. . . But true praise is a worthy sacrifice; this really honors me. Those who walk my path will receive salvation from the Lord" (Psa. 50:13-17, 22-23).

The paths of God are the paths of praise!

5

When Sparrows Fall

"Not one sparrow — (What do they cost? Two for a penny?) can fall to the ground without your Father knowing it. And the very hairs of your head are all numbered. So don't worry! You are more valuable to him than many sparrows" (Matt. 10:29-31).

Jesus told his disciples that our Father in heaven keeps an eye on every sparrow and counts every hair on our heads; yet the fact remains that sparrows *do* fall. Tragedies *do* come to us. Innocent little children die under the wheels of cars driven by drunks. Someone we love is struck by cancer and dies in spite of our fervent prayers.

Could God have prevented the sparrow's fall? The tragedy? The child's death? The spread of cancer?

Most of us believe that God has the power to prevent such things *if* He wants to. We are then left to wrestle in our minds with the problem of *why* God permits what seems to us to be the triumph of evil over good.

Sometimes we draw the conclusion that God is calloused, uncaring, or partial; or we think that the victims of evil *suffer* because of their own or someone else's sin. Both conclusions are in stark contrast with the Good News of the Bible that tells us God is love, and we don't have to be good to deserve His loving care.

It is impossible to praise God for *all* things if we think that

He is not really responsible for everything that happens, or that He is sometimes indifferent to suffering.

Often I receive letters from people who ask me if it is right to thank God for something that is evil, when the Bible tells us to hate evil. They quote, "Ye that love the Lord, hate evil" (Psa. 97:10 KJV) and "Hate the evil, and love the good" (Amos 5:15 KJV).

What is meant here is that we are not to approve of evil, practice evil, embrace evil, or submit to evil.

Praising God for evil circumstances does *not* mean that we approve of evil or accept evil for evil's own sake, except in the sense that Paul spoke of taking pleasure in pain — not for the sake of pain itself, but because we *know* that God is at work in and through it.

God did not create evil, because God is love. But God created beings with free will and the capacity for evil. Evil came about as a consequence of man's rebellion, and it remains in this world with God's permission, but is always subject to His will. Nothing evil can come near us without God's permission.

Because evil does exist, God sent His Son to die on the cross to break the power of evil in the lives of all who would believe in Him.

"The evil bow before the good," says Prov. 14:19 (KJV).

We who believe have been given the power to overcome the world.

"Every one who believes ... that Jesus is the Christ ... is a born-again child of God ... whatever is born of God is victorious over the world; and this is the victory that conquers the world, even our faith" (I John 5:1,4 *Amplified Bible*).

So what is this faith to be grounded on? What are we to believe in order to overcome? We believe in Jesus Christ, but there is more to that package. To fully believe in Jesus Christ also means that we accept that God is the all-powerful God He says He is and that nothing happens without His knowledge or outside His will.

If we set ourselves to firmly believe this, and so praise God for every circumstance of apparent evil around us, I am convinced that *every* difficult situation, *every* tragedy, will be changed by the hand of God.

When I say this, I know that most of you will jump to the conclusion that God is going to change a situation to what *we* think is good. But that is *not* what I am saying.

When we fully trust an evil situation or condition to God, thanking and praising Him for it, the power of God will change, override, or overcome the intention and plan of the evil power inherent in the situation, transforming it to fit with the *original*, perfect intention and plan of God.

We may not understand God's plan or recognize it as good, but when we praise Him for it, we release His power to work in the situation for our good.

(Our ideas of good and bad are often sadly distorted. For instance, if a child inherits a million dollars, we say, "How wonderful!" But if a child dies and goes home to heaven, we say, "How tragic!" Yet we know that a million-dollar inheritance can lead to tragedies, while going home to heaven can only be good.)

If we praise God in all circumstances, I believe that some sparrows will be prevented from falling, some little children will not die, some cancers will be halted and leave. Yet this is *not* to be our motivation for praising God. Some sparrows will still fall, some children will die, and some people will succumb to cancer. Our praise must be *for* these instances also.

We are told to praise God for bringing evil into our lives, trusting that He has a plan and purpose with it, but what are we supposed to do next? How do we personally react to evil when we come face-to-face with it. There is a lot of fuzzy thinking on this point among Christians.

Jesus told his followers, "Resist not evil" (Matt. 5:39). Yet we read that when He saw merchants selling cattle, sheep, and doves and exchanging money in the temple area, He "made a whip from some ropes and chased them all out, and drove out the sheep and oxen, scattering the money changers' coins over the floor and turning over their tables!" (John 2:15).

Here we see Jesus taking overt action against evil. Yet He did not resist the men who came to arrest Him in the Garden of Gethsemane, and He reprimanded the disciple who tried to defend Him with a sword.

So there is a time that God would lead us to take overt action against a force of evil; other times He would have us submit without resistance. How do we know when to do what?

I think our only recourse here is to recognize that in ourselves we have no power to overcome evil. The overcoming power is always God. The essence of God's message to us is that we must learn to focus our attention on Him, the source of overcoming power, and not direct our attention toward the evil confronting us. He will then direct our action moment by moment.

Paul told the Romans, "Do not let yourself be overcome by evil, but overcome (master) evil with good" (Rom. 12:21 *Amplified Bible*).

In the case of Jesus' arrest and crucifixion, it was His very act of nonresistance to evil that broke the power over evil in the world.

Jesus was showing us that there is a better way to deal with evil than to resist it in the sense that we think of resistance. Our idea of resistance is to react in kind, using force against force, and so we react to the evil circumstances opposing us, rather than responding to God's presence and guidance in the situation.

Anytime our action is prompted by the evil circumstances surrounding us rather than by our faith in God's power and perfect control of the situation, we're allowing evil to overcome us, rather than overcoming evil with the power of God.

Jesus was not a pacifist. When He said, "Resist not evil," He meant that we should instead *actively* recognize the power of God over evil and recognize that God sometimes chooses to use apparently evil circumstances to bring about His plan of good.

In such a case, to resist evil would mean that we were working to thwart God's perfect plan. If the disciples had succeeded in preventing the arrest of Jesus in the Garden of Gethsemane, they would have meddled in God's plan, although it would have seemed to them that they were scoring a victory over evil.

Jesus came to conquer, not to teach us how to lose without whimpering.

Both James and Peter tell us to stand firm in faith against Satan. If we look at the context of their message, it is clear that they are in complete agreement with Jesus and with Paul.

"So give yourself humbly to God. Resist the devil and he will flee from you. And when you draw close to God, God will draw close to you" (James 4:7). "Be careful — watch out for attacks from Satan, your great enemy . . . Stand firm when he attacks. Trust the Lord . . . (I Pet. 5:8-9).

Our only defense against the power of Satan is the power of God. That power is released when we stand firm in our faith that God is in perfect and loving control of every detail of the circumstances surrounding us. We express that faith in praising and thanking Him for the situation.

We are told to be careful and watch for the enemy's attack, but our attention must be focused on God, not on Satan. We are to be aware of our enemy, but our protection doesn't lie in watching the enemy, but rather in our knowledge of God's power.

If we let fear and doubts and a preoccupation with the presence of evil take over our minds, we block the power of God from entering the situation. We must learn to see evil in the right perspective — subject to the mighty power of God — and then let that power work everything for good according to God's perfect plan.

Our part is to stand firm in faith, obedient to the promptings of the Holy Spirit, who will guide our outward actions in the situation. Inwardly, our part is *always* to keep our eyes on God and to praise and thank Him for His goodness and mercy in all things.

Standing firm in *faith* means that we must set our will to decide to accept God's Word that He is in charge, regardless of what our feelings or outward circumstances may be like.

The Bible firmly states that God is in charge of every rainstorm, earthquake, tornado or hurricane, every war, famine and pestilence, every birth or death, every flower in the field, every sparrow, and every hair on our heads. We will have to decide whether or not to believe Him all the way.

Some people say, "I can see that God is responsible for some things, but I can't accept that He is in charge of everything.

This is not an adequate basis for praise, and in the particular areas where we refuse to see God's hand, we can never expect to see an answered prayer or evidence of His transforming power.

Let us see what the Bible has to say about some areas where we have difficulty recognizing the hand of God.

Habakkuk was a prophet who complained about the conditions of his country much like some of us complain about the world today.

"O Lord, how long must I call for help before you will listen?" Habakkuk cried. [He didn't even think God was listening, and I'm afraid there are modern-day Christians who agree with him.] "I shout to you in vain; there is no answer. 'Help! Murder!' I cry, but no one comes to save. Must I forever see this sin and sadness all around me? Wherever I look there is oppression and bribery and men who love to argue and to fight. The law is not enforced and there is no justice given in the courts, for the wicked far outnumber the righteous, and bribes and trickery prevail" (Hab. 1:2-4).

Have you ever looked at twentieth-century America and voiced those thoughts? I have.

God answered the prophet, "Look, and be amazed! You will be astounded at what I am about to do! For I am going to do something in your own lifetime that you will have to see to believe. I am raising a new force on the world scene, the Chaldeans, a cruel and violent nation who will march across the world and conquer it!" (Hab. 1:5-6).

God said that *He* would raise up a cruel and violent nation to conquer the world. Do you think any of the armies we've seen rise on the world scene since then came up any other way?

God didn't just *allow* the Chaldeans to conquer, He *raised* them up. What about Napoleon? Hitler? What about the Communist armies of Russia and China? Are we willing to thank God for raising them up? Can we accept His word that He is doing it for our good? Can we honestly praise Him for it?

84

Habakkuk was shocked when he heard what God intended to do.

"O Lord my God, my Holy One," he cried, "you who are eternal — is your plan in all of this to wipe us out? Surely not! O God our Rock, you have decreed the rise of these Chaldeans to chasten and correct us for our awful sins. We are wicked, but they far more. Will you, who cannot allow sin in any form, stand idly by while they swallow us up? Should You be silent while the wicked destroy those who are better than they?" (Hab. 1:12-13)].

Have you ever wondered why God allowed evil and cruel men to hurt innocent ones? I have.

Habakkuk continued, "Are we but fish, to be caught and killed? . . . Must we be strung up on their hooks and dragged out in their nets, while they rejoice? . . . Will you let them get away with this forever?" (Hab. 1:14-15, 17).

God didn't turn a deaf ear to Habakkuk's questions, but told him to write down the answer for all the world to see and remember.

"These things I plan won't happen right away. Slowly, steadily, surely, the time approaches when the vision will be fulfilled. If it seems slow, do not despair, for these things will surely come to pass. Just be patient! They will not be overdue a single day!" (Hab. 2:3).

God is never late! His timing is perfect, but we are always fussing because our estimates are wrong.

"Not this," God told Habakkuk: "Wicked men trust themselves alone [as these Chaldeans do], and fail; but the righteous man trusts in me, and lives" (Hab. 2:4).

The Chaldeans would fail in the end; they would be betrayed by their own arrogance, carried away by their own greed. Their apparent glory would turn to shame, as the consequences of their evil would catch up with them until the time would come that all the earth would be filled with an awareness of the glory of God.

Now Habakkuk saw the greatness of God's plan, and he cried out in triumph, singing to God.

"O Lord, now I have heard your report, and I worship you in awe for the fearful things you are going to do . . . I see God moving across the deserts . . . His brilliant splendor fills the earth and sky; his glory fills the heavens, and the earth full of his praise! What a wonderful God he is! From his hands flash rays of brilliant light. He rejoices in his awesome power. Pestilence marches before him; plague follows close behind. He stops; he stands still for a moment, gazing at the earth. Then he shakes the nations, scattering the everlasting mountains and leveling the hills. His power is just the same as always!'' (Hab. 3:2-6).

Habakkuk was awed by the vision he had seen. He no longer questioned God's control over the fires, earthquakes, pestilence, famines, and wars. Habakkuk's lips quivered with fear, his legs gave way under him and he was shaking in terror, but he sang to God, "Even though the fig trees are all destroyed, and there is neither blossom left nor fruit, and though the olive crops all fail, and the fields lie barren; even if the flocks die in the fields and the cattle barns are empty, yet I will rejoice in the Lord; I will be happy in the God of my salvation. The Lord God is my Strength, and he will give me the speed of a deer and bring me safely over the mountains" (Hab. 3:17-19).

Habakkuk trembled in terror at the vision God had shown him of the future, but he also realized that God was a God of love, justice, and mercy, and he didn't hesitate to trust himself completely into His hands, praising Him for His perfect plan for Israel.

God's command to us is that we praise Him, too — even if our lips tremble in fear and we shake in terror over the outward circumstances of His plan for us.

Through the prophet Isaiah, God told His people that He intended to raise up King Cyrus of Persia to conquer and crush many nations. King Cyrus didn't know God, but God intended to use him to bring the Jewish captives home from Babylon and rebuild the temple and Jerusalem.

Why would God choose Cyrus, a heathen king, to carry out His purposes? To those who would question Him, God answered, "I form the light and make the dark. I send good times and bad. I, Jehovah, am he who does these things . . . Woe to the man who fights with his Creator. Does the pot argue with its maker? Does the clay dispute with him who forms it, saying, 'Stop, you're doing it wrong!' or the pot exclaim, 'How clumsy can you be'? ... Jehovah, the Holy One of Israel, Israel's Creator, says: What right have you to question what I do? Who are you to command me concerning the work of my hands? I have made the earth and created man upon it. With my hands I have stretched out the heavens and commanded all the vast myriads of stars. I have raised up Cyrus to fulfill my righteous purpose, and I will direct all his paths ..." (Isa. 45:7, 9, 11-13).

When we refuse to see God's hand in every situation around us, we are like the pot arguing with its maker. We say "Now if *I* were God, I certainly wouldn't do it *that* way. I wouldn't send an earthquake to Peru or let that little girl die of leukemia or allow that preacher to thunder untruth from the pulpit, leading gullible people astray ... and I certainly wouldn't allow heroin-pushers to tempt little children!"

God knows how we feel about these things and how limited our understanding is. He spoke through the prophet Isaiah:

"This plan of mine is not what you would work out, neither are my thoughts the same as yours! For just as the heavens are higher than the earth, so are my ways higher than yours, and my thoughts than yours. As the rain and snow come down from heaven and stay upon the ground to water the earth, and cause the grain to grow and to produce seed for the farmer and bread for the hungry, so also is my Word. I send it out and it always produces fruit. It shall accomplish all I want it to, and prosper everywhere I send it" (Isa. 55:8-11).

Our skepticism and disappointment in God's plan is rooted in a distrust of God. We're not convinced that He has our best interest in mind.

We question why it is necessary for an innocent child to die under the wheels of a car driven by a drunk in order that the driver come to recognize his need for God. Does God care more for the soul of the drunken driver than He does for the child or the child's grieving parents?

We all ask countless questions like that, turning them over and over in our minds, and while we are torn by the questions, we have no peace and the situation remains unchanged.

The only way out of our dilemma is to accept God's Word on faith. Faith, in spite of what we think, feel, or see. His Word is that He loves us, and that the death of an innocent child *does* fit into God's loving plan for each of the lives affected.

God's love for us can be accepted only on faith, just as we accept every other promise in the Bible. We must decide to believe in the nature of His love, because He says it is so, regardless of whether we *feel* loved or not.

The Good News of the Bible is that God loves us with a love more kind, more patient, more long-suffering and concerned with our happiness and well-being than any human love can be. God loves us and has a perfect plan for our lives. He sent His Son to die for us, to provide us with a new life full of abundant joy and peace, in a world filled with suffering.

We can't possibly understand, with our limited human understanding, the magnificent scope of God's plan for us and for this world. Like Habakkuk, we are shocked that God intends to use earthquakes and wars, suffering and death to bring His plan about.

But God's plan is a perfect plan. It is the only plan that has ever worked on this earth where mankind's rebellion and evil has prevailed. Look at the bloody mess we've made in trying to order our own lives throughout history.

God's plan is not what we would work out, He told Isaiah, because His thoughts are so much higher than ours, His perspective so much higher.

God wants only what is best for us.

"You will live in joy and peace. The mountains and hills, the trees of the field — all the world around you will rejoice. Where once were thorns, fir trees will grow; where briars grew, the myrtle trees will sprout up. This miracle will make the Lord's name very great and be an everlasting sign [of God's power and love]" (Isa. 55:12-13).

God wants to shower us with blessings. He wants to take care of us in every way, down to every little detail of our daily lives. Yet we insist on looking at all the circumstances, the outward workings of His plan, and speculate on what they mean and how they all fit in, while His command to us is that we look to Him and trust Him.

We make our understanding into a wall between us and God as long as we insist on figuring out and approving His plan before we dare trust ourselves to Him.

Here, just as in our first approach to God, acceptance of His will and plan must come before understanding. We must deliberately set aside our own desire for knowledge and comprehension of what God is doing, and throw the weight of our will into a decision to trust His Word.

His plan for us is good. Can we trust His Word for that?

His plan for Job was good, but it was a plan that tested Job's faith to the utmost and staggered his understanding.

Job was a good man. In fact, God said of him, "He is the finest man in all the earth — a good man who fears God and will have nothing to do with evil" (Job 1:8).

So what happened to Job? He lost everything he had. His cattle, his crops . . . and one day the roof fell in and killed all his children.

If that happened to you or to one of your neighbors, would you say it was God? Or Satan?

In Job's case it *was* Satan. But how did it come about? Satan came to God and asked His permission to bring the troubles on Job.

Satan may be the actor who acts out his role in the drama of our life, but God is still the Director.

So what was Job's response? He fell down on the ground before God and tore his clothes in grief.

"I came naked from my mother's womb . . . and I shall have nothing when I die. The Lord gave me everything I had, and they were His to take away. *Blessed be the name of the Lord!*" (Job 1:21).

But that wasn't the end of Job's troubles. Satan came and asked permission once more to torment Job, and God gave it.

This time Job was struck with boils all over his body, until he became so disfigured that no one could bear to look at him. His own wife told him to curse God and die, and his neighbors, who had always respected him, now mocked him and turned away. Three of his best friends, who came to tell him that his suffering was caused by his sins, advised him to repent.

89

Job never doubted that God had brought his misfortune. He cried out for mercy, but was convinced that it was not his sins that had brought about his suffering. Job knew in his heart that he was a righteous man, and he trusted God.

"Though he slay me, yet will I trust in him: I am going to argue my case with him" (Job 13:15 KJV and *Living Bible*).

Job's faith that God was in charge never wavered, but his understanding questioned God's purpose and methods. Job's questions have been echoed by all of us, at one time or another.

"Why do you allow poverty, God? Why do you allow the innocent to suffer? Why are evil men living in ease and comfort? Why don't you listen to my plea? God, why don't you let me die so my sufferings will end and I can rest with you?"

When God answered Job, it was the stern rebuke of a Father to a son.

"Where were you when I laid the foundations of the earth? Tell me, if you know so much ... Have you ever commanded the morning to appear, and caused the dawn to rise in the east? ... Where is the path to the distribution point of light? Where is the home of the east wind? ... Can you hold back the stars? ... Can you ensure the proper sequence of the seasons? ... Who gives intuition and instinct? Who makes the wild donkeys wild? ... Have you given the horse strength, or clothed his neck with a quivering mane? ... Is it at your command that the eagle rises high upon the cliffs to make her nest? ... Do you still want to argue with the Almighty? Or will you yield? Do you — God's critic — have the answers?" (Job 38:4, 12, 24, 31-32, 36; 39:5, 19, 27, 40:2).

Job replied, "I am nothing — how could I ever find the answers? I lay my hand upon my mouth in silence. I have said too much already" (Job 40:4-5).

God continued His impressive list of His creation: the animals, their ways and strength, God's power over all men.

"Who can stand before me? I owe no one anything. Everything under the heaven is mine!" (Job 41:10-11).

Job replied, "I know that You can do all things and that no thought or purpose of Yours can be restrained or thwarted ...

90

I was talking about things I knew nothing about and did not understand, things far too wonderful for me . . . I had heard of You only by the hearing of the ear; but now my (spiritual) eye sees You . . . I loathe myself and repent in dust and ashes'' (Job 42:2-3, 5-6 *Amplified Bible* and *Living Bible*).

The Lord spoke harshly also to Job's three friends who had totally misunderstood the reasons for Job's suffering. God told them they had been wrong and instructed them to offer up a burnt offering and then have Job pray for them.

The three men did as they were told, and ''when Job prayed for his friends, the Lord restored his wealth and happiness! In fact, the Lord gave him twice as much as before'' (Job 42:10).

It is interesting to note that God blessed Job when Job had blessed those who had accused him wrongly. Job had learned his lesson. No longer would he question God's operation of the universe. No longer would he see or hear with his natural senses only, but with his new, spiritual insight.

God had a perfect plan for Job. His trials were executed by Satan, but permitted by God to give Job greater faith and wisdom, and to show him just how great and loving God is.

God had a perfect plan for Ruth, the Moabite. Yet it looked for all the world as if misfortune followed her. First she lost her husband. Then she went with her mother-in-law back to Bethlehem and they were so poor that Ruth had to go into the fields of the rich farmers and glean whatever was left after the harvest. That doesn't sound like the outworking of a wonderful plan, does it? But Ruth trusted God, and there in the field she met Boaz, a rich relative of her dead husband. Boaz fell in love with Ruth and they were married. God's plan had worked, and Ruth became the grandmother of King David.

Or what about God's perfect plan for Joseph? God planned that Joseph would become Pharaoh's right-hand man in Egypt, because God intended to use him, at just the right time, to save the nation of Israel from famine.

Joseph was sold by his brothers as a slave to a caravan of merchants on their way to Egypt. It was the first step in God's plan, but Joseph's brothers had no idea that they were serving God's purpose. They hated their brother and meant only to harm him.

Later Joseph became the trusted servant of an influential Egyptian, and it looked as if he was on his way up the social ladder. But he was falsely accused of attempting to rape the Egyptian's wife and was thrown in jail. If that happened to you, would you think that the devil had won a victory? Or would you have accepted it as part of God's perfect plan?

It was in jail that God arranged for Joseph to meet Pharaoh's butler and interpret his dream. Joseph asked the butler to plead with Pharaoh to pardon him, and the butler promised, but forgot all about it. Joseph spent another two years in jail, and that surely looked like an unfortunate quirk of fate. But God's timing was perfect. Pharaoh dreamed a strange pair of dreams that no one could interpret. Suddenly the forgetful butler remembered the fellow he'd met in jail a couple of years before. Joseph was brought before Pharaoh, and God told Joseph the meaning of Pharaoh's dreams. Seven years of bountiful harvests would be followed by seven years of severe famine. Pharoah accepted the interpretation of his dreams, and appointed Joseph to be in charge of the ingathering and storage of grain during the seven rich years, and in charge of the distribution of food during the seven lean years to follow.

When Joseph's brothers came to Egypt to buy grain, he revealed his identity, and they fell down before him, stricken with fear and remorse. But Joseph said, "Don't be angry with yourselves that you did this to me [sold me into slavery], for God did it! He sent me here ahead of you to preserve your lives ... It was God who sent me here, not you! ... As for you, you thought evil against me; but God meant it for good, to bring about that many people should be kept alive, as they are this day" (Gen 45:5, 8; 50:20 *Amplified Bible* and *Living Bible*).

God *meant* it for good! We often will admit that God is able to make all things work out to good for us, the way the Bible says, but we think that God takes whatever happens to us and makes the best of it, sort of a secondhand blessing. But God isn't on the defensive. He isn't limited to making the best out of a bad situation. *God has the initiative!* We need to remind ourselves of that every so often.

God had the initiative when Stephen was stoned to death (Acts 7). Stephen was a man, full of the Holy Spirit, who served the Lord faithfully. When he was stoned to death, Saul of Tarsus, an angry young persecutor of Christians, was among the spectators.

Stephen obviously trusted that God was completely in charge of the situation, for he knelt down while the stones were being hurled at him, and cried out with a loud voice, "Lord, don't charge them with this sin!" And then he died. Stephen knew that although persecutors meant evil against him, God meant it for good.

Would you be able to thank God for the murder of the most Christlike Christian man you know and believe He was using the seeming tragedy for some great good?

Saul of Tarsus became Paul the apostle after a remarkable conversion experience on the road to Damascus. He experienced his share of what looked like mishaps in spreading the gospel.

Once when Paul and Silas came to Philippi, they were accused of corrupting the city and were stripped and beaten with wooden whips until the blood ran from their bare backs. Then they were put in the inner dungeon of the prison with their feet clamped in stocks. (Acts 16:20-24).

But Paul and Silas didn't think that Satan had won a victory or that God has deserted them. They were convinced that God had called them to preach in Philippi, and that He was working in everything to bring about His perfect plan for them. So they didn't whine or complain or cry out to the Lord for help. They sat there in the dungeon with the blood stiffened on their sore backs, unable to stretch their aching legs, and they were praying and singing hymns of praise to God.

Suddenly, at midnight, there was a great earthquake, the prison doors flew open, and the chains fell off every prisoner. The jailer was horrified, thinking they had all escaped, and drew his sword to kill himself. But Paul yelled out, assuring him that all the prisoners were there, and the jailer came and threw himself down before their feet. "What must I do to be saved?" he begged.

Beginning with the jailer and his entire family, the people of Philippi received the Gospel (Acts 16).

God had a perfect plan for the city of Philippi. He sent Paul and Silas to be His witnesses there, and they had faith to believe that God was working out His plan, even if He used circumstances they could not have anticipated.

We are always trying to anticipate what God will do. Because He worked out a set of circumstances one way once, we draw the conclusion that He will do the same thing in every similar set of circumstances. But Paul wasn't always dramatically released from prison. Sometimes he stayed there for years.

Paul suffered many afflictions. He was stoned and left for dead, shipwrecked, bitten by a snake, suffered disease and persecution ... but never once did he think that God had stopped directing every incident of his life. He counted it all for joy and an opportunity to praise God. Paul knew that his suffering was working *for* him.

For years I suffered with excruciating headaches. In vain I searched the Scriptures, clinging to God's promise of healing, but I couldn't find a clue to the reason for my agony, nor did it go away.

In the meantime, I was tormented with doubts. Over and over I allowed myself to speculate *why* this particular suffering had come my way. The thoughts whirled in my head. *"Why doesn't God do something about your pain? You're praying for others who get healed, but your own pain is still with you.*

As I suffered and tossed through long, sleepless nights, the thoughts persisted. *Look how miserable you are! If God is a just God who knows about your suffering —, He surely wouldn't hold it against you if you ended your life. Just be careful how you do it, and no one will suspect suicide; no one will be hurt, and you'll be free from the pain ...*

Like the arguments of Job's friends, these thoughts can sound very reasonable when you are racked with pain. But of course, they are a bunch of lies, invented by the master deceiver, Satan himself, who comes near only by permission of God.

Our accuser and tormentor must flee when we draw near to God and take our stand on His Word of truth.

My headaches didn't suddenly go away, but I determined to believe that God wouldn't permit anything to happen to me unless it was for my good. Therefore, the headaches had to be for my good, and I began to praise and thank God for them every time they came. As I did, something wonderful began to work *for* me. The more I hurt, the more thankful I became, and with the thanksgiving I experienced a new depth of joy radiating through my entire being.

Richard Wurmbrand tells what happened when the physical pain and mental agony of a Communist prison became more than he could bear. Three years of solitary confinement and torture was threatening to rob him of his sanity, but as he reached the extremity of his endurance, Richard Wurmbrand still trusted God and praised Him for His everpresent mercy and love. Wurmbrand tells how, at this point, joy began to radiate through his being, filled his cell.

God meant his suffering for good. Richard Wurmbrand's ministry is now influencing the entire world *because* of what he suffered.

"As for God, his way is perfect," said the psalmist: "the word of the Lord is tried: he is a buckler to all those that trust in him" (Psa. 18:30 KJV).

The way may lead through fierce battles, through raging storms, or fire or flood; yet everywhere, God's presence goes with us, and His hand guides us, says the Bible.

How can we doubt it? He created the soldier and his weapons, the storm, the fire, and the waters of the flood. They are all under His perfect control.

Why did God cause a storm on the lake when Jesus was there in a boat with His disciples? Only so that His power and authority over the storm could be demonstrated (Mark 4).

Why did God cause a man to be blind from birth?

Jesus and His disciples were walking along when they saw a man blind from birth. " 'Master,' his disciples asked him, 'why was this man born blind? Was it a result of his own sins or those of his parents?' 'Neither,' Jesus answered. 'But to demonstrate the power of God.' " Then Jesus went on to heal the man (John 9:2-3).

The disciples looked at the blind man from the viewpoint of human reasoning and understanding; Jesus saw the situation under the perfect control and power of God.

Our viewpoint makes all the difference.

I've received hundreds of letters from people who've read *Prison to Praise*. Seventy-five percent of the letters come from people who tell me how they've started praising God for a difficult situation, with amazing results. Twenty-five percent of the letters come from people who tell of the same kinds of situations, but they are not able to believe that God is at work and can't praise Him for it. They are defeated, discouraged, and desperate.

The difference is not in the situation, but in the viewpoint, and consequently in the outcome.

Many write about the death of a close friend or relative.

"Tom suffered so terrible," wrote one lady. "We had taken him to healing services and prayer groups all over the country. He seemed better for a while, and our hopes soared. Then the cancer came back, and after months of agony he died. How could God be so inconsistent? I can't believe it was His will that Tom die so young. He was a Christian and wanted to serve God. If God did it all just to teach the rest of us a lesson, why did Tom have to suffer? I can't believe I'm supposed to praise God for what has happened."

Here is another letter:

"Charles accepted Christ less than a year ago. He was a radiant witness for the Lord. After six months he developed cancer. He had two operations, but the growth in his lungs returned. He called the elders of his church; they anointed him and prayed for his healing. When he went back for his checkup, the growth had disappeared. Charles rejoiced and praised the Lord. Then a few months later he had severe headaches. He went into the hospital for a checkup and was dead in two days. Brain cancer.

"A Pastor friend of the family flew in to preach at the funeral. On the plane he sat down next to a youth. They began to talk; the pastor shared Charles's story and the young boy gave his life to Jesus Christ before the plane landed. In new Orleans the pastor changed flights. On the next leg of his journey he sat next to a young woman. She, too, inquired where he was going, and he told her the story about Charles. Before the plane landed, she had accepted Jesus Christ as her Savior. The funeral was an occasion to praise the Lord for all He had done in Charles's life. After the funeral, two men accepted Christ on the sidewalk outside the chapel. Charles's body was flown to his hometown for burial. During the ceremony, I couldn't take my eyes off the face of the young widow. She was radiant with an inner peace and joy. During the past year she and Charles had come to know the joy in praising God for all things. She told me, 'Death is swallowed up in victory' (I Cor. 15:54). I have no reason to weep. Praise God!''

The two letters told of similar circumstances, but what a difference. One is a story of defeat, the other of victory. One sees from the human viewpoint, the other from the viewpoint of Christ.

The Bible tells us that we *can* have the viewpoint of Christ.

"Let this mind be in you, which was also in Christ Jesus" (Phil. 2:5 KJV). "And be constantly renewed in the spirit of your mind" (Eph. 4:23 *Amplified Bible*).

Paul wasn't suggesting an impossibility. The key words in his passages are "let" and "be renewed". We cannot give ourselves the viewpoint of Christ, but God will renew our minds if we *let* Him.

If we are willing to let it happen, we can tell God and expect Him to bring it about. Our part then is to *believe* it has happened.

David wanted to be in oneness with God's will for his life, yet he knew he couldn't change his own rebellious heart. He cried out to God: *"Remove* from me the way of falsehood and unfaithfulness (to You), and graciously *impart* Your law to me. I have *chosen* the way of truth and faithfulness; Your ordinances have I set before me ... I will [not merely walk, but] run the way of Your commandments, when *You give me a heart that is willing"* (Psa. 119:29-30, 32 *Amplified Bible*).

David knew that the only action within his power was to choose to will the right way. God had to remove the wrong and impart the right and give David a willing heart.

God will do the same for us if we choose to let Him, then stand firm in faith, believing it is done. Whatever circumstances come into our lives, we are to praise and thank God for them, because they are His way of working out His perfect plan for us. The circumstances are His way of removing the wrong, imparting the right, and giving us a willing heart.

Praise releases the power of God into our lives and circumstances, because praise is faith in action. When we trust God fully, He is free to work, and He *always* brings victory. It may be a victory that changes circumstances, or a victory *in* the circumstances. Death may be turned away, or made to lose its sting.

Praise is a permanent acceptance of what God has brought into our lives. We enter this attitude of praise by an act of our will, by a decision to praise God regardless of how we feel.

"What time I am afraid, I will ... trust ... You," wrote David. "By [the help of] God I will praise His Word; on God I lean, rely and confidently put my trust" (Psa. 56:3-4 *Amplified Bible*).

My heart is fixed, O God, my heart is fixed: I will sing and give praise" (Psa. 57:7 KJV).

6

Good-bye Grumblings

Have you ever stepped outside your door on a beautiful, clear, sunny day, taken a deep breath of fresh air, and thanked God for His wonderful creation?

But what if the next morning is gray and rainy? Does it automatically make you feel a little depressed as you look out the window? Maybe you don't say it out loud, but how do you feel?

Are you in the habit of thanking God only for what you want? And are you in the habit of grumbling just a little when things don't go the way you like?

So what's wrong with a little complaining? It's no big thing. What difference does it make?

It makes *all* the difference in the world. *Everything* depends on how we respond to the little things in life.

A marriage counselor will tell you that a marriage usually breaks up over little things. It takes only a small nail to puncture a tire. A small mistake by a mechanic can cause the crash of a giant airliner. A misunderstanding can start a war. One angry word leads to a shooting. Little things mean a lot, because this is the level where we live, down at the nitty-gritty of our attitude at the breakfast table, or in the long check-out line at the supermarket on a Friday afternoon.

Grumbling comes so easy to all of us that we often don't

realize what we're doing. But grumbling is the very opposite of thanksgiving; a complaint is the opposite of trust; a murmur against your wife when she burns your toast is the opposite of loving acceptance.

The dictionary defines a complaint as an accusation. By complaining and grumbling you are actually accusing God of mismanaging the details of your day. The attitude of praise releases the power of God into our lives, and the attitude of murmuring and complaining blocks that power.

"And don't murmur against God and his dealings with you, as some of them did, for that is why God sent His Angel [of death] to destroy them. All these things happened to them as examples — as object lessons to us — to warn us against doing the same things; they were written down so that we could read about them and learn from them ... "(I Cor. 10:10-11).

Paul was speaking about the behavior of the Israelites on their wanderings from Egypt to the Promised Land. So what did they do and what were the terrible consequences?

"The people were ... complaining about all their misfortunes, and the Lord heard them. His anger flared against them because of their complaints ... " (Num. 11:1).

Moses had led the Israelites out of Egypt, and God had given them some remarkable signs of His presence and concern for them. He had parted the Red Sea, allowing them to walk across on dry land, and later brought the water back over the heads of the Egyptian soldiers pursuing them. God promised to lead His people to the Promised Land; He promised to feed them in the wilderness, and to drive their enemies out before them — if they would only trust Him. As a sign, God's presence went with them in the form of a pillar of dust in the daytime, and a pillar of fire at night.

But the Israelites didn't trust God. They complained bitterly, first because of a lack of food and water, and later because they didn't like the taste of the water God gave them. They grew tired of the diet God had provided for them. They fussed and complained about petty little things. And what were the consequences?

Patiently, God humored His murmuring children. Again and again He met their needs, until it became obvious that they would not learn. When they got tired of the taste of manna, and wanted meat instead, God said that He would give them meat, not just for one day or two days, but for a whole month, "until [you are satiated and vomit it up violently, and it] come out at your nostrils, and is disgusting to you; because you have rejected and despised the Lord . . . " (Num. 11:20 *Amplified Bible*).

Forty years the Israelites wandered and every time something went wrong, they complained bitterly and wanted to go back to the fleshpots of Egypt.

Why did it take them forty years to cover less than two hundred miles? Even with women and children and cattle, they could have covered the distance in a few weeks. They were delayed because they murmured and refused to trust that God would keep His promise to take care of their every need.

When the Israelites first came to the border of their Promised Land, they discovered that giants already lived there, in fortified cities. Instead of rejoicing at the obstacles, praising God who had promised to drive all their enemies out before them, the Israelites turned against Moses and demanded to be taken back to the fleshpots of Egypt. They accused Moses of having tricked them and fooled them.

Only two men, Joshua and Caleb, who had seen the giants and the fortified cities, trusted that God would keep His promise and give the Israelites the land. But no one listened to Joshua and Caleb.

This was the last straw. God vowed to let the Israelites stew in their own complaints. Not one of the complainers would live to set foot on the Promised Land. Instead, the nation of Israel would wander in the wilderness for forty years, until a new generation would be grown up. *They* would be allowed to enter, led by Joshua and Caleb, the only two who would survive the wilderness years.

"God was patient with them for forty years, though they tried his patience sorely; he kept right on doing his mighty miracles for them to see. 'But,' God says, 'I was very angry with them, for their hearts were always looking somewhere else instead of up to me, and they never found the paths I wanted them to follow' " (Heb. 3:10).

Petty complaining kept the Israelites out of their Promised Land.

Our complaints and murmurings against God in the little things can keep us from entering into the perfect plan He has for our lives.

"Beware then of your own hearts, dear brothers, lest you find that they, too, are evil and unbelieving and are leading you away from the living God" (Heb. 3:12).

The cause of the Israelites' murmuring was unbelief, and unbelief is at the root of every one of our little complaints.

Unbelief kept the Israelites out of Canaan. But God wanted to do more for them than just bring them into a geographical location. God's Promised Land was also to be a place of perfect rest, an attitude of perfect trust and peace of mind.

"Although God's promise still stands — his promise that all may enter his place of rest — we ought to tremble with fear because some of you may be on the verge of failing to get there after all . . . For only we who believe God can enter into his place of rest. He has said, 'I have sworn in my anger that those who don't believe me will never get in' " (Heb. 4:1, 3).

God has a place of perfect rest prepared for us now. And I don't mean after death, I mean *now*. It is that state of perfect trust in Him that we can all enter into on faith. But in order to do so, we must give up our sin of unbelief, our grumblings, murmurings, and complaints. Unbelief is a serious offense against God.

"The world's sin is unbelief in me, " said Jesus (John 16:9).

Unbelief, like all sin, is a deliberate act of rebellion against God. We can choose to believe or not to believe.

Webster defines unbelief as a "withholding of belief: incredulity or skepticism: a rejection of what is asserted."

If unbelief is a deliberate withholding of belief, then we are responsible for our action, and we must do something about it.

The first step in dealing with any sin is confession.

For years I had proudly told myself that I rarely grumbled, that is, I rarely grumbled out loud. I had cultivated and maintained a smiling facade, but I was a habitual grumbler inside. Of course, as long as I didn't think I was guilty of grumbling, I never improved.

I thought *my* kinds of complaints were legitimate. I grumbled when I didn't get enough sleep and had to get out of bed in the morning without feeling rested. I grumbled under my breath if the bathroom was messed up by another member of my family and I grumbled over my hurried breakfast. I grumbled when things went wrong at the office, and when people didn't do what I expected of them. I grumbled over bills, and when my car wouldn't start, or when I hit a red light on my way to anywhere. I grumbled when I had to work late at the office and didn't get to be on time; and the next morning I started all over again.

When finally the Holy Spirit began to show me what the Bible had to say about thanking God in everything, I began to realize that I'd been doing the opposite for years and never thought a thing about it.

The first step toward rehabilitation was to admit to myself that I was a habitual grumbler.

I believe that the most effective way to deal with our sins is to be specific about them. We admit them, confess them, ask God's forgiveness, and make a clear-cut decision not to fall into that sin again. We then ask God to remove the sin from us and to give us increased faith and strength to withstand any temptation. At last we thank Him for it and proceed on faith, knowing that it has been done.

Once we make an agreement with God not to grumble, and promise instead to thank Him for every little thing that used to make us grumble, we can expect Him to go to work.

We can't change ourselves from unbelieving grumblers to thankful, cheerful believers. God has to do the changing. We make the decision to quit grumbling and start thanking and praising God, but it is God's power that works the transformation. Our job is to keep our eyes on Jesus and thank God for what *He* is able to do.

In practice, we will find that God will bring into our lives the very kinds of circumstances that used to trigger our grumbling. When we see them coming, we can thank and praise God, because He's using those very incidents to bring about the change in us. Before, they made us stumble; now they will show us God's strength. They will serve to increase our faith.

Accepting every little thing that happens with joy and thanksgiving will release the power of God in and through us, and we will soon experience a *feeling* of joy as well. But don't look for the feeling as a sign. Our praise and thanksgiving must be based on faith in God's Word, not on our feelings.

One of the things I'd grumbled about for years was my lack of musical talent. Whenever I heard beautiful music, I failed to enjoy it fully, because it always made me wish I could play an instrument or sing beautiful solos.

Then one day I was listening to a concert, and the question came into my mind, "Are you thankful that you can't play a musical instrument?"

I recognized the source of the question as the Holy Spirit and squirmed in my seat.

"No, Lord, I guess I'm not."

"Are you willing to be?"

"Yes, Lord, I'm willing, and I understand that this will be your will for me. You could have arranged to give me a musical talent and have it trained if you wanted to, so I thank you for me, just as you wanted me to be."

As I said it, a great peace flowed into me, and I realized that I was actually happy to be as I am.

"What I wanted you to learn is this," the Holy Spirit said: "If you could make beautiful music, you would please some people, but when you give praise you always please God."

My lack of musical talent was never a shortcoming in God's eyes, only in my own. *I* was the one who was dissatisfied with the way God had made me. He was never dissatisfied.

There are people who spend their lives wishing they could have a special talent and an opportunity to develop it. They grumble and complain inside because they are sure that given the right breaks in life, they might have become a movie star, TV personality, baseball hero, business tycoon, or doctor.

Do you have a favorite grumble about your own life? Do you say to yourself that if you could only have a chance to live it over again, you'd be in a different profession, a different neighborhood, a different marriage?

Can you accept that God has you right now exactly where He wants you? That He hasn't overlooked a thing? That He wasn't helpless to interfere back when you made what you think of as your wrong choice?

Sure, there is such a thing as a wrong choice. We've been talking in the book about our responsibility to choose and the consequences of the right and wrong choices. But the promise of God is that He makes all things, including our own wrong choices, work out for good when we trust Him.

It is possible that you are in a job or in a situation God plans to move you out of. Still, it is essential that *right now* you accept your present situation with joy and thank God for it. As we thank God for every difficulty, submitting to His will at every turn, He is able to move us into the spot where He wants us.

Remember, He was able to move the heathen King Cyrus into the perfect spot at the right time even when Cyrus didn't know God. So you can be sure that if God had wanted you to be somewhere else at this very moment, He would have had you there. Your task right now is to thank Him for where you are at the *present*.

If God, by His Holy Spirit, shows you that you made a wrong choice fifteen years ago when you deliberately chose to go against what you then knew to be God's will for you, confess that wrong choice to Him now, ask His forgiveness, thank Him for it, and ask Him to guide you in making right anything you may have done to wrong others. Then turn the rest of your life, as of this moment, completely over into God's hands and trust that He now is in complete charge. *Now* praise and thank Him for your *present* circumstances exactly as they are in every detail.

You may discover God's power going to work to move you out of your present circumstances very quickly, or you may find that God's power is transforming you in the midst of the circumstances. Whatever happens, continue to thank Him. For He is in charge.

A Christian businessman made a deeper commitment of his life to Christ, and shortly thereafter found himself laid off from his highly-paid job as an executive. The man searched for another job, but cutbacks in the industry made positions scarce. His family suffered from the financial stress, and his anxieties increased as the bills mounted and his prayers seemed unanswered.

He had been unemployed for a year when he heard me speak one Saturday night about being thankful for all things. It suddenly dawned on him that God probably had a good reason for not having led him to a job, and he began to thank God for his unemployment and for every hardship he and his family were suffering as a result.

All day Sunday he continued to praise God, and he discovered that all his fears and resentments concerning the situation were decreasing. In their place, he felt genuine joy.

Early Monday morning the phone rang. Another executive wanted to know if he could go to work for him.

"Yes, I'm available, " said the man.

"How soon can you start?"

"Tomorrow."

"Then be here at 9 a.m., ready to start."

His new job gave an excellent salary, but more important, he was in direct contact with groups of businessmen daily. His witness for Christ led one man after the other to accept the Lord as his Savior.

The businessman told me, "As long as I carried a spark of fear and resentment over my situation, I was blocking God from doing what He wanted to with my life. As soon as I was able to trust Him and praise Him for my life exactly as it was, He was able to take over and place me where He wanted me."

A young teacher was spending her summer vacation in the mountains when a letter was mailed from the superintendent's office telling her to report for a conference concerning next year's assignment. She didn't get the letter, and when she didn't show up for the conference, her job was given to someone else.

When she returned from her vacation, she discovered that she was unemployed.

Her first impulse was to panic and go home to her parents in another state. School was to start in two weeks; there were no job openings in the district; and she had heavy financial obligations from her college days.

This young lady had just read *Prison to Praise* and recognized her present situation as an opportunity to practice what she'd learned. She deliberately quenched the impulse to panic, thanked God that He had allowed her to lose her job, and thanked Him for His perfect plan for her life.

For two days she praised God, fighting back every temptation to despair. On the third day a neighbor talked to her across the back fence.

"You know, you really ought to be teaching in a Christian school," she said. "Why don't you call the principal of the school where my son goes?"

The young teacher did, and discovered to her surprise that a position as first-grade teacher had been left suddenly vacant. She was interviewed and got the job.

"I know that God was able to take over the situation because I trusted Him enough to praise Him, " she said. "If I'd pulled my usual old trick of panicking and running home to Mom and Dad, I might still have been unemployed and fussing at God for not looking after me."

Her new job suited her far better than the old one. She was able to freely share her faith in the classroom, and could openly pray with several of the children who had behavior problems.

God had a perfect plan and a perfect place for the young teacher and for the Christian busnessman. He closed the doors to the jobs they had held and thought they wanted, and He opened the right doors when they trusted Him and praised Him *for* their unemployment.

Resentment and fear, grumbling and complaining, cause delays in the unfolding of God's plan for us. He has a perfect time plan, and we must realize that His timing doesn't always coincide with ours.

I had always been punctual, and was proud of my ability to organize and make proper use of "the Lord's time." Then one day I found myself on a plane enroute to El Paso, Texas, where I was to speak at a convention of businessmen. I was glancing nervously at my watch. It was moving toward 2:30 p.m., and I had planned to be at the meeting at 2:00. *Now what possible good can come out of my being late for an engagement?* I wondered.

"Why are you letting this happen, Lord?" I asked, with just a trace of irritability. The only answer was another question:

"Are you thankful you are late?"

"That's not the point," I argued back. "Those poor people who arranged for me to come, and paid my expenses, are expecting me there on time. They are the ones who'll have to learn to be thankful."

Are you thankful? The thought persisted.

The truth suddenly dawned on me. I wasn't really moved by concern for the people at the meeting. *I* was the one who was upset. *I* wasn't trusting that God was handling the situation right. I was fussing and arguing over His management of "my" time.

"I'm sorry, Lord," I whispered. "I *do* believe you know best how to manage my time. If you're letting me be late, it must be part of your perfect plan, and I thank you for it. I turn the management of my time over to you and trust you to work it out for good."

I leaned back in my seat and drew a breath of relief. My watch said 2:45, but I felt perfect peace. At that moment the stewardess walked past, and her watch came into sharp focus before my eyes. It read 1:45.

I sat up. "Miss, your watch says 1:45. Are you sure that is correct?"

"Yes, sir, it is. We've just crossed into another time zone, and it is now 1:45."

I chuckled to myself. "Thank you, Lord, for teaching me how silly it is to worry about the time."

As the plane flew on, the time moved past 2:00, and I felt a twinge of anxiety again. At 2:15 we were coming in for landing at El Paso, but it looked like I would still be a few minutes late.

"Lord, I'm sorry I'm impatient," I muttered. "But I've never been late to a meeting before, and I don't understand why you're letting it happen now."

"Are you thankful?"

"All right, Lord," I said. "I *will* be thankful. Thank you that it is now 2:20, and I'm exactly where I am."

When I walked off the plane, my watch said 2:25.

I pulled the convention schedule out of my pocket to check on the address, and my eyes fell on the time for the meeting. It said 2:30!

I ran to the nearest cabstand. *This is beautiful, Lord,* I thought. *You've been able to teach me a lesson about trusting your management of my time, without hurting anybody else.* (Incidentally, that is *always* the way God operates. We may think that others are hurt by our mistakes, but God is in complete control of our lives also, and He loves them as He loves us.)

The cabdriver looked at me expectantly. "Where to, Sir?"

"The El Paso Hilton Inn," I gasped. 'I need to get there as quickly as possible!"

The cabdriver chuckled and pointed across the street.

"There it is, right in front of you!"

I walked through the door into the convention hall and glanced at my watch. It was exactly 2:30. The men were walking up to the speakers' table, and I filed up behind them to take my seat.

God's timetable is precise to the minute. How great it is to know that we're on His schedule.

Release the timekeeping of your life to Him. He will get you where He wants you, when He wants you there, if you trust Him. His schedule is good for every appointment and every hour of our lives. God doesn't force His time plan on us, but if we give our days and hours to Him, it is His business to get us where He wants us on His time.

That doesn't mean we can sit down in our soft seats and say, "If the Lord wants me there, He'll have to get me there. I'm just going to sit here and doze until He moves me."

We've got to do our part, but that is *not* to worry about the timekeeping. We do our best, get up on time in the morning, prepare in time for appointments, then thank Him for whatever happens — even if we oversleep, get delayed unexpectedly, or are interrupted by a talkative neighbor or demanding child.

God has a double purpose in teaching us to trust and praise Him in everything. It releases His power into *our* situation, and it also draws others to Him.

I once worked with a choir-leader who was a perfectionist. Every detail of the music for each service was planned and performed with precision, but the choir-leader always performed under a strain, and his tension was transmitted to the choir. They sang with excellence, but without joy.

One day the choir-leader dropped by for a chat in my office.

"Bob, I think you would be more relaxed and experience much joy in your music if you began to thank God for everything that happens." I said.

He looked at me in silence for some time, then said, "I've been watching you these past six months. At first I thought you were putting on a front. No one could be that joyful all the time." He smiled. "I made several mistakes with the choir, and you always reacted with joy . . . I don't understand how you do it, but I'd like to have the same attitude."

We talked until the time for choir-rehearsal, and Bob left my office in a hurry. He hadn't had time for any preparations, and I wondered how he would respond to the unexpected challenge.

Later he told me, "I was getting really tense thinking about all the music and equipment I hadn't prepared, but then it dawned on me: this was exactly the kind of situation we'd talked about thanking God for, so I thanked Him. Just then, four members of the choir came in the door. They were early for rehearsal and asked, "What can we do to help you get ready?" Nothing like that had ever happened in the months I had led the choir.

"I was amazed. 'Thank you, God,' I prayed. 'You really took care of that problem quickly!' "

The rest of the day Bob had wandered in a half-daze. He had never realized before that God was personally concerned with the details of his life, and that God's power would be released as soon as he relaxed and was thankful in every circumstance. The discovery completely changed Bob's attitude to his music ministry.

The next time he sang a solo, he made several mistakes, something that ordinarily would have plunged him into despair. But instead of getting more tense with each wrong note, he offered up thanks to God Who allowed it to happen. As a result, he experienced increasing joy as the song progressed, and we who listened could see the happiness radiate from his face and hear the new dimension of joy in his singing.

Bob's relationship with the congregation also changed markedly. He had been greeting us with a glum "Hello", now he beamed and said, "Good morning! Isn't it a beautiful day!"

Wearing a glum face may not seem like a sin, until we consider the fact that it expresses the very opposite of happy, hopeful faith, and as such is actually an attitude of unbelief.

We all know the expression, "Well, we all have our bad days and our ups and downs." This is careless, dangerous thinking, because it suggests that bad days and ups and downs are a normal part of the Christian life. The Bible says that our *outward* circumstances may go up and down, be bad or good, but our *inner* attitude is to be a permanent state of rejoicing in Christ.

"I have learned how to get along happily whatever the circumstances may be," Paul wrote from a jail cell. "I know now how to live when things are difficult and I know how to live when things are prosperous. In general and in particular I have learned the secret of facing either plenty or poverty. I am ready for anything through the strength of the one who lives within me" (Phil. 4:11-13 *Living Bible* and Phillips).

The consequences of our failure to be thankful in the little things are not always apparent to us, but once I was taught a stern lesson.

It was a busy morning in our chaplain's office at Fort Benning, and everything seemed to go wrong. The senior man in charge had not shown up for work, and none of the others seemed to know what to do. Telephones were ringing, work was piling up, and I began to feel impatient with the man who had not reported for duty. Of course, my attitude didn't make him arrive, nor did it improve the situation. I grumbled under my breath through most of a miserable day.

The next day the man returned and explained that he had gone to the hospital where he was told that he had a cancerous growth in his sinus. Overcome at the news, he had gone home to spend the day in bed, not caring if he ever got up again.

I was overwhelmed with remorse. I'd fussed over the insignificant delays at the office, instead of thanking God for the man who was absent. My grumblings had effectively put me out of commission as a channel for God's love and power flowing toward the sick man that day.

It is important that we learn to respond with trust and praise in all situations, whether or not the consequences are apparent to us. As we learn to push the praise button instead of the panic button, our lives and our attitudes are changed, whether the situation confronting us is a dramatic event or a minor irritation.

Once a man was driving home from work on icy roads. He misjudged the road conditions and slid through a stop sign and into another car. No one was injured, but the cars were badly damaged, and the responsible driver was angry with himself for having made a stupid mistake. Then he remembered having read recently about praising God for everything.

"Thank you for this accident, Lord," he prayed.

Immediately a silent voice whispered in his head, "Don't be stupid. You've made a bad mistake already. Are you going to make it worse by pretending you're glad about it?"

"But God has promised to make it work for good, " he argued back.

"You'll never see anything good come out of *this*!"

"If I thank God, I will," the man persisted.

He continued to be thankful for the accident, yet nothing outwardly dramatic happened as a result. The other driver wasn't led to Christ, and no one seemed to react to his joyful attitude at the garage.

So what difference did it make how he reacted?

As the day progressed, something very remarkable was happening *in* that man. The more he thanked God, the more a new kind of peace spread inside him. Toward noon he discovered that something like bubbling laughter kept welling up from within, and each time he repeated his thanks to God for the car accident, he could feel something being released, like the untying of tight knots, deep within him.

He had been an average Christian but from that day on his life was never again the same. He had entered a new dimension of victorious living in Christ — all because of his determination to recognize God's hand in something he had first thought was his own stupid mistake and a stroke of bad luck.

Another man heard me speak about praising God for everything and promised God from that moment he would be thankful for everything that happened to him.

He and his family drove home from the meeting through a snowstorm in below-zero weather. They arrived home late at night, and the moment they stepped in the front door, they knew something was wrong. The house was ice-cold, and the furnace was dead.

The family huddled upstairs while the man walked down to the basement to check the furnace. He knew nothing about furnaces and had no idea what might be wrong.

He stood staring at the cold, silent furnace, and his first impulse was to pray that God would help him get it going again. Without heat in the house, He would have to take his family to a warm shelter for the night.

Then the thought came to him, "Are you thankful now?"

"I'm sorry, Lord, I forgot," he prayed. "But I know you must have planned this for our good, so thank you, God, for this furnace, just as it is.

At that moment a very distinct suggestion came into his mind: "Check the fan!"

The fan? I don't even know where it is!

"Look behind the plate on the right side," came the thought.

He found a screwdriver and began removing the plate. The whole scene suddenly struck him as ridiculous. Was he just imagining things? Was the fan really behind that plate? But if God was really at work giving him this direct kind of help, he couldn't stop now, he reasoned.

His fingers were numb with cold, but the plate came off — and there was the fan.

Now *what*? he thought.

"Look for the fan belt; it is off."

It was too dark to see inside the furnace, so he got a flashlight and directed the beam down the small opening in the furnace. There was the fan belt, lying loose. He slipped it over the drive shaft on the fan and removed his arm from the narrow opening. The furnace remained cold and silent.

"What now?" he prayed.

"Turn the furnace switch," came the suggestion.

As soon as he turned the switch, the furnace came alive with happy dancing flames, and the man ran upstairs to share with his family how God had blessed them with a cold furnace.

Had the man *not* responded to the crisis by praising God and expecting Him to work it all for good, he and his family would have suffered inconvenience and hardship. The cold furnace was a God-given opportunity to learn in practice that praise releases the power and guidance of God.

Following the furnace incident, that man's life was changed. He began to listen for the voice of God in all situations, and today has developed a rare sensitivity to the promptings of the Holy Spirit. His open ear to the guidance of God has made him a channel for God's power in the lives of others also.

The first step was an act of faith, believing that a cold furnace on a dark, snowy night was an expression of God's loving concern for his and his family's welfare. He could have passed up that first opportunity, and I am sure that God would have provided other challenges. You and I are confronted with opportunities to recognize God's hand in every situation of our daily lives. How many opportunities do we pass up?

The results of our reactions are cumulative. With each positive step of faith, it becomes easier to believe. In the same way, each time we allow unbelief to deny God's presence and love in a difficult situation, the negative results heap up, and it becomes increasingly difficult to muster our will to exercise any faith at all. The more we grumble, the more we become entangled in the web of defeat. Many little grumbles add up to overwhelming mountains of depression.

A Christian nurse wrote of years she had spent in misery.

"It seemed like little things always upset me and caused

irritation. Gradually my life was getting more and more miserable. I prayed for God to help me, but nothing happened. I started taking pills to get going in the morning and pills to go to sleep at night. Every day began with the agony of having to get out of bed. I couldn't cope with my own housework. At the hospital I was breaking under the strain of caring for the patients.

"Every day was worse than the one before. I couldn't even do little things I had been able to do with ease a few months before. I was sinking into such a depression that I prayed for God to let me die. Living was sheer hell."

Then one day she read *Prison to Praise*.

"It was like a light of hope had been turned on inside me," she wrote. She determined to praise God for everything, and made a long list of things to be thankful for, beginning with the circumstances that had caused her so much strain. The results soon began to show up.

"All I can think of now is, *What a wonderful change in my life there has been — since Jesus came into my heart!* I no longer have a horrible fear of failure hanging over me. Things don't irritate and upset me. When something appears to go wrong, I just look up and say, 'Thank you, Lord!' and it really puts a song in my heart!"

Whether you are surrounded by what seem to you like mountains of accumulated misery, or just irritating little molehills, the turning point is the same. Confess your complaining and murmuring as a sin, and promise God that you'll be thankful from now on.

You make the decision and determine to stand on it in faith; God will furnish the strength to do it. Once you've made your commitment, the opportunities to thank God may come in little or big packages, but they'll come.

At a retreat near Fort Benning, several young people made a promise to thank God for all things. The next day one of the soldiers was notified that a favorite uncle had been killed in a tractor accident on the farm. Immediately the thought came to the soldier, "Now see what happened! You made that silly commitment to praise God. Your uncle wasn't even a Christian!"

115

The soldier recognized the source of that thought, and resisted the temptation to complain to God about his uncle's death. Instead he prayed, "God, you know how much I loved my uncle, but you loved him more, so you must have had a good reason for letting him die. I'll just thank you and praise you for doing what was best."

The soldier felt a peace about his uncle's death, but was unable to shake off a concern for his cousin who had just recently accepted Christ as his Savior. How would he take his father's death? The soldier wanted to go home for the funeral in order to encourage his cousin, but he was unable to get leave.

"Okay, God," he prayed. "You know all about my cousin, so I'll just thank you that I can't go." He thought he would call home and ask his parents to convey a message to his cousin, and stepped into a phone booth to make the call.

When a voice answered at the other end, he immediately recognized his cousin. "How are you? " he blurted out in surprise.

"I'm praising the Lord," came the answer. "We're all so glad that Dad accepted Christ several days before the accident. He had time to tell everybody what God had done for him, and we know it was God's will that he go to heaven now."

The soldier returned to the retreat to share with the others what had happened. A chaplain's wife who was there promised God she would thank Him for everything in her life.

Driving home that evening, she had her first opportunity. In eighteen years of driving, she'd never had a traffic ticket. This time she was asked to pull over to the side of the road and an MP who'd been following her at a distance gave her a ticket for going through an intersection without making the required stop.

She explained to the MP that he had made a mistake. Another car looking just like hers had failed to stop at the intersection, speeding past her as she came to a careful halt. The policeman did not accept her story, and her first impulse was to be angry and complain about the injustice. Then she remembered her promise to be thankful in everything.

"God, I trust this is your will," she prayed. "I will praise you for the whole experience." Suddenly she discovered that her inner being was flooded with joy.

The next day she returned to the retreat and told us what had happened.

"Isn't it marvelous?" she said, "We don't have to worry about being treated unfairly or taken advantage of. Even *those* circumstances become a source of joy and strength when we see God's hand in them and give thanks."

Others are drawn to Christ when we praise God. If we grumble and complain as bitterly as our non-Christian friends over the many little upsetting incidents of our days, others conclude that our faith does no more for us than having no faith does for them. Unless they can see, in the nitty-gritty of our daily lives, that Christ makes a difference, how can we expect them to believe when we say they need Jesus?

It isn't what we say, but what we are and what we do that draws others to the Christ-life in us. Nowhere is this more apparent than in our daily lives. How do we react to delays and difficulties on the job, in emergencies, in everyday encounters? Do we react in such a way that no one sees anything different about us? Or does our reaction cause them to stop and say, "Something is different about that person. He's got something I need"?

One couple read *Prison to Praise* and were convinced that God wanted them to be thankful for everything. One night they were awakened at 2:30 a.m. by the sound of breaking glass. The man looked outside and saw that all the windows in his car had been smashed by a group of kids who were fast disappearing around the corner.

The couple agreed that God had given them an opportunity to praise Him, and they knelt by their bed, giving thanks for what had happened.

The next morning the man took his car to a garage and explained what had happened.

"Thank God," he said. "I'm sure He has a wonderful purpose behind it all."

The owner of the garage shook his head.

"If something like that happened to me, I'd see to it that those young punks were made to pay," he said.

117

The customer smiled. "That isn't necessary," he explained. "God is in charge of the situation; I don't need to be upset about it."

The garage-owner stared at him for a moment, then said, "I've been a Christian for years, but I never heard about praising God for vandalism."

They talked on, and the customer told the garage-owner about the baptism in the Holy Spirit and the power of God released through praise.

"Hold it," said the garage-owner. "I've heard about the baptism in the Holy Spirit till I've gotten sick of it. I have one customer who talks about nothing else. But tell me more about praising God. That sounds interesting."

The customer explained that he thought the two subjects were one, since both had to do with complete trust and commitment to God. Finally the garage-owner accepted an invitation to attend a meeting of Spirit-filled businessmen, and at the meeting he experienced the baptism in the Holy Spirit for himself.

Next he committed himself to praising God for everything, and the first item on his list was his business. It had been sliding toward bankruptcy for two years.

The next afternoon one of his employees came with bad news; he had been in an accident, wrecking their truck. This could be the last straw, toppling the business.

The garage-owner looked at his young employee, who stood pale and trembling, obviously expecting an outburst of temper from his boss. Instead the garage-owner smiled, put his arm around the young man's shoulders and said, "Let us praise God for this accident and believe He will work it out for good!"

A routine insurance claim was submitted, and to the garage-owner's amazement, the settlement enabled him to pay urgent bills. The accident marked the turning point in his business, and his profits began to show a marked increase. It marked an even more important turning point in the life of the garage-owner who now experienced increasing joy and peace in every area of his life. In turn, a steady stream of customers came to know Jesus Christ as their Savior because they were impressed with his obvious joy.

When the joy of Christ is released in our lives, others are drawn to Him.

Once, after a late meeting, I walked into a restaurant and asked for a glass of milk. The waitress smiled and went to the kitchen to get my order. A moment later she reappeared with an angry frown on her face.

"I'm very sorry, sir, but someone has locked the refrigerator, and I can't get any milk for you."

"Thank the Lord!" I responded automatically. The waitress looked puzzled.

"Why did you say that?"

"I have learned to be thankful for everything, because I believe that God works everything for good if you let Him."

"What religion are you?" she asked incredulously.

"Methodist."

"Well, I'm a Baptist, but I have never heard of being thankful for things like that!"

"Are you a Christian Baptist?" I asked.

"Well," she hesitated, "I think I am, but I've never been sure."

"You can be absolutely sure," I said. "Jesus came into the world to give us eternal life as a free gift. All we have to do is ask Him to forgive our sins and then believe that He does. I'd like to pray with you and ask God to give you this free gift if you want it."

The waitress nodded eagerly. "Yes, sir, I would like that!"

I touched her shoulder with my hand, we bowed our heads, and there in the empty restaurant, a few minutes after midnight, I prayed that God would release her faith and give her assurance of eternal life through Christ.

Tears were running down her face.

"I've never felt like this before in my life, " she said. "I feel as if a great burden has rolled off my back. I really do believe I'm a Christian now."

It may seem inconsequential to make a point out of being grateful for not getting a glass of milk when you want it, but as you learn to thank God for every little thing, God will use your praise to draw unhappy, weary people to Him. And He can turn their burden of worries and anxieties into pure joy and peace.

119

I was sitting in an Atlanta airport, waiting to board a plane, when a stranger suddenly picked up the briefcase I had placed on a low table beside me. I had left the latch open, and the contents spilled all over the floor. Papers flew in all directions, and I noticed my toothbrush, thrown out of its case, lying on the dirty floor. I stifled the impulse to be upset with the clumsy stranger and muttered under my breath, "Yes, Lord, I do thank you for this and I know you have some good reason for letting it happen."

The embarrassed stranger apologized and hastily began to pick up my scattered belongings. When I joined him, he looked up and said, "You don't remember me, do you?"

"No, I'm afraid I don't."

He explained that we had met briefly several months ago and that he had just now been walking through the terminal feeling tired and discouraged, asking God to lead him to someone who could help.

"I saw you and picked up your briefcase in order to sit down on the table next to you," he explained. "Now I know God led me to you. Will you please explain how you could remain completely undisturbed when I spilled your things all over the floor?"

I was more than happy to tell him how glorious it is to trust that all things work for good if we love God, and that little experiences like an upset briefcase are opportunities to thank God and watch Him work.

The man was amazed and asked several questions. When the time came for my plane to leave, he said, "Would you consider coming to Fort Lauderdale, Florida, as my guest, at your earliest convenience?"

It was my turn to be amazed. I had been praying that God would provide a way for me to go to Fort Lauderdale. I had heard much about what God had been doing in the lives of Christians there.

Paul wrote to the Christians at Philippi:

"In everything you do, stay away from complaining and arguing, so that no one can speak a word of blame against you. You are to live clean, innocent lives as children of God in a dark world full of people who are crooked and stubborn. Shine out among them like beacon lights, holding out to them the Word of Life ... Whatever happens, dear friends, be glad in the Lord. I never get tired of telling you this and it is good for you to hear it again and again'' (Phil. 2:14-16; 3:1).

It is our lack of complaining and our happiness in Christ that enables us to shine like beacons, holding out the Word of Life in a dark world. It was true in Philippi, and it is true today.

Let's quit our grumblings and praise the Lord for every dark and crooked thing we see around us. Do it, and watch God's light penetrate the darkness.

7

The Joy of the Lord

"The joy of the Lord is your strength, " said the prophet Nehemiah (Neh. 8:10).

No wonder Jesus was so concerned that His disciples would understand that He had come, not only to purchase their salvation through His sacrifice on the cross, but also to provide them with the sustaining power of His joy.

"You haven't tried this before," He told them, "[but begin now]. Ask, using my name, and you will receive, and your cup of joy will overflow" (John 16:24).

The joy of the Lord is ours for the asking!

Jesus prayed for us: "That *My joy* may be made full and complete and perfect in them — that they may experience *My delight* fulfilled in them, that *My enjoyment* may be perfected in their own souls, that they may have *My gladness* within them filling their hearts" (John 17:13 *Amplified Bible*).

Every born-again Christian knows that his salvation is a free gift. He was born again of the Holy Spirit when he accepted Jesus Christ as his Savior, *on faith*. Many Christians have come to discover that there is more to God's free gift than just being born again as a child of God. The baptism in the Holy Spirit, can be claimed *on faith*. But very few of us seem to have realized that Jesus has already provided us with His joy. It is there to be claimed *on faith* with the rest of the package.

If the joy of the Lord is our strength, then it is obviously not something that comes last in a long line of attainments, sort of like the whipped topping on the cake. It is something we need for the start, something to sustain us and strengthen us in our task of carrying the Good News around the world.

Paul wrote to the Corinthians, "When I come although I can't do much to help your faith, for it is strong already, I want to be able to do something about your joy: I want to make you happy, not sad" (II Cor. 1:24).

Paul didn't mean that He would *make* them happy by bringing nice gifts or providing pleasant circumstances. He intended to remind them of the joy they had already been given. He wanted them to practice rejoicing to cultivate the joy planted in them by the Holy Spirit.

Paul knew that the outward circumstances for an active Christian witness would always be filled with trials and suffering. His source of joy was his inward abiding in Christ.

"The Holy Spirit clearly ... affirms to me in city after city that imprisonment and suffering await me. But none of these things move me; neither do I esteem my life dear to myself, *if only I may finish my course with joy,* and the ministry which I have obtained of ... the Lord Jesus faithfully to attest the good news ... of God's grace ..." (Acts 20:23-24 *Amplified Bible).*

If joy has already been given us by Jesus, why do most Christians live such joyless lives?

Jesus prayed that His joy would be perfected in us. What He means is that we can't make ourselves joyful anymore than we can save ourselves, give ourselves peace, or make ourselves more loving. What we *can* do is to choose to accept and trust what Jesus has done for us and allow Him to perfect His joy in us.

In practice, this means that we deliberately set out to practice joy, regardless of how we feel, trusting that God then goes to work, transforming our sorrows into pure joy, just as He has promised.

Love, joy, and peace are all part of the fruit of the Holy Spirit in us. Jesus told his disciples how they were to cultivate this fruit.

"I have loved you even as the Father has loved Me. Live within my love. When you obey me you are living in my love, just as I obey My Father and live in his love. *I have told you this so that you will be filled with my joy*" (John 15:9-11).

The source of joy was not to be found in happy circumstances, but in knowing Jesus' commandments, obeying them, and abiding in Him.

Jeremiah wrote, "Your words were found, and I ate them, and Your word was to me a joy and the rejoicing of my heart" (Jer. 15:16 *Amplified Bible).*

Joy is certainly something we are meant to feel. It is to be a happy, overflowing, pleasant experience. But joy does not depend on feeling. We are not to rejoice because we feel joyful, rather we can expect to eventually feel joyful as a result of our rejoicing.

David had learned the secret of rejoicing. "Rejoice with trembling," he wrote in Psa. 2:11. "And now shall my head be lifted up above my enemies round about me; in His tent will I offer *sacrifices* and *shouting of joy*; I will sing, yes, I will sing praises to the Lord" (Psa. 27:6 *Amplified Bible.*)

For a long time I thought that joy was something I would experience when I was satisfied and things were happy around me. Now I realize that joy doesn't spring up in my emotions, but is triggered by my will and is part and parcel of the life of praise.

"Let all the joys of the godly well up in praise to the Lord, for it is right to praise him, " wrote David in Psa. 33:1.

Joy, thanksgiving and praise belong together, and our commitment to praise and thank God for everything does not become complete until we've committed ourselves to rejoice in everything as well.

An elderly woman who had been filled with the Holy Spirit and had been an active Christian worker for years became crippled with arthritis. Years of pain had robbed her of any joy in living; the smallest household chore was an agony, and she experienced increasing depression.

She believed that God could heal, and had gone to healing meetings, but her condition only grew worse. One day she heard about the power in praising God for everything, and made up her mind to try it. Her task wasn't easy, since now every moment of her days and nights was filled with pain. But she was willing to be genuinely thankful for every part of her life, including her pain.

One day she moved slowly across her kitchen floor, carrying a tray of utensils. Suddenly the tray dropped, scattering items over the entire floor. Her painful back and stiff fingers made it impossible for her to bend over to pick anything up from the floor. Her usual reaction to dropping an object was to break down in tears of self-pity. But this time she remembered her promise to praise God.

"Thank you, Lord," she prayed, "for letting me drop everything on the floor. I believe you're working it to my good."

In a flash she became aware of other beings in the kitchen besides herself. She had been alone — yet now she sensed others present. Startled, she realized she was surrounded by angels. The angels were laughing and rejoicing, and she knew their joy was for her. Suddenly she understood.

Jesus told His disciples, "There is rejoicing among the angels of God over one sinner whose heart is changed." (Luke 15:10 Phillips).

She was certainly a saved sinner whose heart had been miraculously changed. For years she had been filled with self-pity and complaint against God for letting her suffer. She had begged Him to heal her, and inwardly had felt that God had let her down. At last she had seen that her grumbling was rooted in unbelief, and there was rejoicing among the angels when she trusted God enough to praise Him for the mishap with the tray of utensils.

She stood in the middle of her kitchen floor and felt herself saturated by the joy that filled the room. With a heart rejoicing she could thank God sincerely for allowing the suffering that had brought her such joy.

A short time later she attended a service where they offered prayer for the sick. Confidently, she walked forward. Always before, the painful awareness of her disease had crippled her ability to believe. Now her faith was not anchored in her feelings. She was free to believe, no matter how intense her pain was. That night she was instantly healed. All pain left, and the twisted joints became straight and whole.

We are such creatures of habit. For so long we've let our senses dictate our reactions. But Christ came to live in us so that His joy can become full and complete in us.

The initiative to rejoice can't come to us from our emotions, mind or senses, but from the part of us that is spirit, born of the Holy Spirit. That's where our will resides, and the more we allow our will to take the initiative for our action, rather than giving in to our senses, the more we'll discover that we become increasingly able to respond to any situation with praise, joy and thanksgiving. Our old dependency on feeling will grow weaker, and as we persist, we'll discover that the joy originating in our will and spirit will spread to our senses as well.

What is begun as an act of obedience to God's Word, will eventually bring about in us a state of being where we sense, feel, think, and experience a real, overflowing praise, thanksgiving and joy beyond anything we've ever known.

When we fully submit to God's will, so that all obstacles in us can be flushed away, and we can be molded, transformed, and renewed into perfect vessels for Him, then we'll also find that the joy of the Lord *is* complete in us.

For nearly twenty years I suffered with stomach trouble. Many foods gave me extreme discomfort. I'd gone the rounds of doctors and taken all kinds of medicines, but nothing helped.

I prayed and tried to believe that God would heal me, with no apparent result. Others prayed for me — Christian leaders well-known for their effective ministry in healing, prayer groups, and friends — but the problem continued.

I claimed the promise Jesus gave in Mark 16 that not even poison could hurt me, and frequently ate whatever foods were served to me. But "apparent disaster" struck again and again, and I would be miserably ill, unable to sleep, and feel extremely sorry for myself.

I finally decided to accept on faith the fact that I had been healed by Christ's death for me, and to believe that the symptoms would go away when He was ready. For several years I rested on that assurance and thanked God for working in my life in this way for whatever good He wanted to accomplish.

Before I retired from the army, the doctors decided to operate on my stomach. They found nothing obvious to explain the years of pain I had gone through, and consequently could do nothing to improve my condition.

As I lay in my hospital bed after the operation, the pain increased in severity beyond anything I had endured before. Pain-killers or drugs had no effect. Hour after hour I lay without sleeping, feeling as if the darkness of the room was closing in on me. I thought I could almost reach out and touch the dark power of evil hovering around me, and I fought against the temptation to give in to the terror I felt. I didn't want to die but dreaded living in such misery.

At the moment when the blackness seemed darker than ever, I cried out, "Lord, I don't care what happens or how miserable I am, I thank you for this entire experience. I know you are going to bring something good out of it."

Instantly the darkness of the hospital room was shattered by a brilliant, white light, brighter than the sun. It was as bright as the light I'd seen in a vision several years before. At that time, the Holy Spirit had explained the vision to me. There was a dark cloud hovering over a sunny meadow, and above the cloud was a bright, white light. Up above the cloud was the state of joy and blessing Christ had already secured for us, but to get there, we had to climb on a ladder straight through the dark cloud of confusion and pain. Inside the cloud it was impossible to know what direction to take through the use of our ordinary sense-perception — sight, hearing or feeling. The ladder could only be climbed on faith, and by praising God each step of the way. Climbing through that dark cloud, we would be stripped of our dependency on our senses and learn to trust God's Word. The ladder of praise would lift us right up into the heavenlies, to take our place there with Christ Jesus.

As I lay on my bed in the hospital room, my entire body flooded by that wonderful, brilliant light, I suddenly realized that what had once been a vision, now was a reality.

The years I had walked by faith, believing that God was using my pain for good, were years of climbing through the cloud of darkness and uncertainty. Without the cloud, I would never have learned to let go of my reliance on my senses and feelings. Now I could wholeheartedly thank God for every circumstance of my life that added to the dark cloud. How else could I have learned to utterly trust in Him? How else could I have come to experience this beautiful saturation of light and joy?

When I returned home from the hospital, I discovered that God had done something about the condition of my stomach as well.

The foods that had once sent me into hours of pain no longer bothered me. I rejoiced in my new freedom to eat strawberries, apples, bananas, ice cream — all the things I had tried to stay away from for years.

Over the years, others had been healed instantly as I prayed for them, but God had chosen to strengthen my faith by letting me trust in His Word.

Praise does release the power of God to heal, but the healing is of secondary importance. As long as we're primarily concerned with our own comfort, our desire to be healed and free from physical pain, we've got the wrong perspective. Our concern actually amounts to a questioning of God's plan for us.

For years I'd been afraid of one day losing my teeth. Then one day my dentist told me that my gums were badly infected, and the bones around my teeth were deteriorating. X-rays showed the sad picture; I would soon lose my teeth!

Downhearted, I left the dentist's office. Of course I knew that I ought to be thanking God for my condition, but I wasn't very happy about it.

"Thank you, Lord," I said. "I'm grateful that you've allowed my teeth to get into such bad shape. I'm sure you know better than I do what's best for me, so I praise you, Lord."

Even as I prayed I began to feel more thankful, and when a friend came along, I told her about my new occasion to praise the Lord.

"Have you prayed for healing?" she asked.

"No," I said. "I've just now realized that losing my teeth isn't anything to fuss over, since it can't happen unless God allows it."

"I think God wants you to have perfect teeth," my friend said, placing her hand lightly on my shoulder. "Dear God," she prayed. 'Thank you for letting Merlin's teeth get in such a rotten shape. We praise you and ask that you be glorified in this, so touch Merlin now and heal him completely."

Three days later I was back in the dentist's office and watched while he studied my new X-rays carefully. He had a concerned, puzzled look on his face, and once put the X-rays down to take another look in my mouth. He shook his head and muttered under his breath, and I thought, *Maybe they're worse than he expected.*

Finally the dentist stepped back, looked me over from head to foot, and asked, "What in the world have you done to your teeth?"

"Not a thing!"

"Then I don't understand." He looked from my old X-rays to the new ones. "Your bones are perfect, your gums are no longer infected and swollen — in fact your whole mouth looks perfect!"

I chuckled. How wonderful to know God had healed me — but even better, healing was no longer the real issue. That little gnawing fear I'd carried with me about having false teeth was gone. I knew that with or without perfect teeth of my own, it was a perfect union with Christ and trust in God's loving concern for every detail of my life that really mattered.

Recently I had a letter from a dear lady in New Hampshire. She lives alone with her teen-age son, and when she wrote me, she had been flat on her back and in constant pain after two major operations. She wrote:

"Praise God for His great faithfulness! I was very discouraged after my last operation, but someone gave me *Prison to Praise*. I decided to praise God for my illness and keep looking to Jesus. Since then my pain has not gone away, but I have come to know my Savior in a deeper way, and the Holy Spirit has ministered to me so wonderfully.

"Some of my friends have told me that God made me suffer in order to punish me. But I know this isn't so. Jesus has never accused me; instead He has taught me much about His love. These past months He has used His Word to show me things in my heart and life that shouldn't be there, feelings and thoughts unlike Christ. God in His wonderful love has forgiven me and healed every scar of old hurts in my life.

"I've learned to thank Jesus for the hard places, and even for the pain. I love Jesus with all my heart. I don't understand why He leads the way He does, but if I can be happy and 'take pleasure' in my infirmity (II Cor. 12:10), and in going this way for God, I certainly praise Him for it.

"I have to go back to the hospital for a possible third operation. I thank God for it, knowing that He will work in it for good. I know He can heal me, and I thank Him for whatever He decides in His love is best for me."

Her letter overflowed with genuine joy and gratitude. Her physical body was still in pain, but she had experienced a healing of her emotions and inner being and had entered into a wonderful relationship with God in Christ. Everything else, even her healing, had become secondary.

Oneness with God in Christ was the goal Paul was pressing toward. Jesus knew that His purpose for coming to earth was to remove the sin barrier between man and God, so that once more the Creator could be united with His creation, just as He had originally intended.

Before His crucifixion Jesus prayed for us:

"I am not praying for these alone, but also for the future believers who will come to me because of the testimony of these. My prayer for all of them is that they will be of one heart and mind, just as you and I are, Father — that just as you are in me and I am in you, so they will be in us, and the world will believe you sent me. I have given them the glory you gave me — the glorious unity of being one, as we are — I in them and you in me, all being perfected into one — so that the world will know you sent me and will understand that you love them as much as you love me. Father, I want them with me — these you've given me — so that they can see my glory. You gave me the glory because you loved me before the world began! O righteous Father [Father of goodness and truth], the world doesn't know you, but I do; and these disciples know you sent me. And I have revealed you to them, and will keep on revealing you so that the mighty love you have for me may be in them and I in them" (John 17:20-26).

Jesus prayed, and we know for certain that His prayer was answered. Paul assured us that we *have* been seated with Christ. Christ dwells in us. We are one in Him with the Father.

When we begin to grasp the full significance of these accomplished facts, everything else in our lives begins to take on the right perspective. The outer circumstances that once loomed out of proportion to our relationship with Christ and captured most of our attention can now be seen fitting perfectly into the plan that God is working in our lives. We still don't see the plan, but we *do* see Jesus Christ as Lord and Master, and we *know* that God has a plan and it is good.

Many letters have come to me from people in prisons and penitentiaries across the country since *Prison to Praise* was published.

One fellow wrote from death row:

"I've been sentenced to die in the electric chair. I know I have to die, and for a long time I had no hope for anything beyond death. Fear controlled all my thoughts, and I felt forsaken by God and man. Then I read *Prison to Praise*. It was as if my mind had become alive again. I dared believe that God is for real and is working in every life to draw us to accept His Son as Savior and Lord.

"I looked back on my own sordid life and realized that everything had happened with God's permission so that I might come to the point of reaching out for Him. I did reach out, and in one blinding instant I knew that God does work in all things for our good and His glory. For the first time I knew that my entire life was being blessed by God, and that by faith in His Son I belonged to Him. Now I am truly free and filled with His peace and joy.

Another prisoner wrote:

"I had learned to hate everyone and everything. No matter how hard I tried, I couldn't see any reason to be glad I was alive. Someone gave me *Prison to Praise*, and when I first read it I thought it was a bunch of nonsense. But the more I thought about it, the more I was tempted to try thanking God for my messy life. After all, I was at the bottom; what did I have to lose?"

132

"I began to go over the events of my life, one by one, as they came back to my memory. I thanked God that each incident was a part of His plan for me. The whole program seemed pretty foolish, but I forced myself to keep going. As I stuck with it, something began to happen inside of me. I began to think of God being personally involved in my mixed-up life. Could it really be true that He was interested in *me*? Events I'd forgotten pounded their way back into my mind. I'd thought of them as tragic before; now I began to see them as part of God's faithful drawing to convince me that I needed Him.

"I praised Him for every detail of my life; I thanked Him for the people who had hated me, mistreated me, lied about me, and betrayed me. I thanked Him for the ones I had hated, mistreated, lied about, and betrayed.

"A glowing peace began to flood me. God was healing all the bitter memories. The prison walls melted, and peace surrounded me instead. The walls and the bars can't make me a prisoner anymore. I'm free in Christ, praise God!"

Another letter came from a Christian in a top-security penitentiary in the West:

"Praise God! Attendance at our church and evening Bible-study groups is swelling. Last week three men accepted Christ as their Savior. Imagine what it would mean if three souls came to Jesus every week inside these walls! [A later letter told that in the next month twelve men accepted Christ and four received the baptism in the Holy Spirit.] We really appreciate the prayers of the brothers at Fort Benning. The Lord is making His presence felt in this institution like never before ... God is answering our prayers and we will someday see many souls belong to Jesus among the prisoners here. What a blessing it has been to read *Prison to Praise*. We rejoice over the possibility of a tape-ministry inside the prison walls so that we can actually hear some of the teachings of our Christian brothers on the 'outside'.

"God is so great! Eight years ago I walked through these prison gates with a fresh ten-to-eighty year sentence for armed robbery. I thought my future held nothing but a policeman's bullet or oblivion through alcoholism. I had tried all rehabilitation programs, but when I went out on parole I was drunk for a solid three months and twenty-five days until I was put back in prison. I'd honestly tried to change myself, but it was no use.

"Then six months ago, in an instant, Jesus Christ did the changing for me. I was transformed, just like it says in the Bible. 'Therefore, if any man is in Christ, he is a new creation; the old has passed away, behold, the new has come' (II Cor. 5:17 RSV). Since then, Jesus Christ has been working to clean up my life, letting His light shine over all the murky, cobwebby corners. Praise God! Nobody has a rehabilitation program worthy of mention, compared to the one Christ has to offer. Man cannot change the inner man, only Christ can!

"Praise the wonderful Jesus. He poured over me the light of God's love. The joy of living with Jesus becomes deeper day by day.

"Thank you for joining us in prayer for a continuing awakening among the prisoners, and for a strengthening of the new converts ... Love from the brethren in Jesus."

That Christian brother is living and praising God in circumstances most of us would call dark and difficult. Yet for him, the perspective has become totally changed. He knows the joy of abiding in Jesus Christ, and everything else in his life has become secondary. He has learned to "rejoice evermore. Pray without ceasing. In every thing give thanks: for this is the will of God in Christ Jesus concerning you" (I Thes. 5:16-18 KJV).

John Wesley wrote in his comments on that passage, '*Rejoice evermore* — in uninterrupted happiness in God. *Pray without ceasing* — which is the fruit of always rejoicing in the Lord. *In everything give thanks* — which is the fruit of both of the former. This is Christian perfection. Farther than this we cannot go; we need not stop short of it. Our Lord has purchased joy as well as righteousness for us. It is the very design of the gospel, that being saved from guilt, we should be happy in love of Christ. Thanksgiving is inseparable from true prayer: it is almost essentially connected with it. He that always prays is ever giving praise, whether in ease or pain, both for prosperity and for the greatest adversity. He blesses God for all things, looks on them as coming from Him, and receives them only for His sake; not choosing nor refusing, liking nor disliking anything, but only as it is agreeable or disagreeable to His perfect will" (*Notes on the New Testament*).

To live a life in uninterrupted happiness in God, looking on every circumstance as coming from God, and thanking Him for it — that is Christian perfection.

There is nothing haphazard about God's plan for our lives. Nothing, absolutely nothing, however strange, inconsistent, or evil it may seem to us, happens without God's specific consent.

One lady wrote me her amazing story illustrating that point.

She had been born with only one hand, and from the time she was old enough to realize that she was different from other children, she had worn a scarf or a stole over the stump of her arm to hide her handicap. She was always painfully conscious of her deformity, and as a young woman she began to drink to hide her hurt.

She was fifty-six years old at the time she wrote me:

"Six months ago I visited my sister, and she played a tape where you spoke about praising God for every problem or tragedy in your life. As I listened, I felt like someone had hit me in the stomach. I felt sick. After all the years I'd blamed God for my misfortune, I wasn't ready to thank Him for it. I said 'Lord, forget it. I thanked You for freeing me from alcohol, but I can't thank You for this other thing.'

"But no matter how hard I tried, I couldn't get the thought of thanking God off my mind. It bugged me day and night. Finally I said, 'Lord, why don't you get off my back — I'll do anything for you, but not that! I just can't.' Still, I couldn't find any rest. At last I played the tape once more. This time I heard something I'd missed before. You said that when the young soldier and his wife found themselves *unable* to thank God for the terrible thing they were threatened by, they at last said they were *willing to try*. The rest seemed to come easy. About that time, I'd reached the point where I was willing to try almost anything, just to get some rest. So I told God I was *willing* to try, even if I was sure I wasn't *able*. As soon as I'd

135

said it, it seemed like a load of many years just rolled off my shoulders. I started to praise the Lord — my tears flowed — and it was like the song says, 'Heaven came down and glory filled my soul!' In the middle of all this rejoicing, the Lord spoke to me and said, 'Wait a minute; I'm not through with you yet!' I sat up. What possibly more could there be? I'd just made the supreme sacrifice and thanked God for the deformity I'd hated all my life! But very clearly the words formed in my head:

" 'You are not to carry a stole or a scarf over the stump of your hand anymore!'

"I felt an instant tightening-up inside. 'No, Lord,' I muttered. 'That's going too far. Don't ask me to do that.'

" 'As long as you're hiding it, you're not really thankful; you're still ashamed,' came the gentle reproach. Tearfully, I conceded.

" 'I'm willing to try,' I promised. 'But You've got to make me able.'

"The next time I had occasion to leave the house was when I was called for jury duty. I dressed and automatically reached for my stole. Instantly the warning came. 'No. No!'

"I said, 'All right, God, I'll start out without it, but I am not going to promise I won't come back for it!'

"For the first time in my life I stepped outside the front door without the protective covering to hide my missing hand. As soon as I closed the door behind me, all embarrassment, the shame, and the sense of guilt were washed away! I knew for the first time in my life what it was like to be really free. I knew that God loves me just as I am. Praise the Lord!"

God permits every circumstance of our life for a good reason. Through it, He intends to bring about His perfect and loving plan for us. God permitted that lady to be born without a hand because He loves her. God permitted Satan to harass Job because He loved Job. God permitted Christ to hang on the cross because He loved His Son, and He loved us. God allowed the darkness and evil forces of this world to gain an *apparent* victory — apparent to our senses — yet all the while God's perfect plan for the salvation of the world was being worked out.

No one knew this better than Jesus. Some readers have written me, stating that Jesus complained when He hung on the cross and cried out, "My God, My God, why hast thou forsaken me?"

But to think that Jesus complained is in complete contradiction with everything Jesus said and did about His crucifixion.

No one knew better than Jesus every detail of God's plan to save the world. Jesus had often told his disciples about His coming crucifixion and resurrection, and He had quoted for them passages from the Psalms and Prophets fortelling His sacrifice on the cross. Jesus even urged His disciples to rejoice over what was to happen.

"Remember what I told you," He said. "I am going away, but I will come back to you again. If you really love me, you will be very happy for me, for now I can go to the Father, who is greater than I am" (John 14:28).

He had also told them that no one could take His life without His consent.

"The Father loves me because I lay down my life that I may have it back again. No one can kill me without my consent — I lay down my life voluntarily. For I have the right and power to lay it down when I want to and also the right and power to take it again. For the Father has given me this right" (John 10:17-18).

The disciples had been told the real truth, but when the going got rough, they reacted to the apparent victory of evil and rushed to defend Jesus against the soldiers who came to arrest Him.

Jesus stopped them. "Put away your sword," He said. "Don't you realize that I could ask my Father for thousands of angels to protect us, and he would send them instantly? But if I did, how would the Scriptures be fulfilled that describe what is happening now?"(Matt. 26:52-54).

Jesus knew that God's Word, the Scriptures, must be fulfilled. *No* circumstances or action on our part can change the final outworking of God's Word. Jesus Himself was subject to the Word, although He *is* the Word become flesh.

The Jews who surrounded the cross where Jesus hung were familiar with the passages in the Old Testament foretelling the coming of their Messiah who would be crucified for their sins.

The words Jesus cried out, "My God, my God, why hast thou forsaken me?" were the introductory words to the well-known Psalm 22, a psalm of praise and victory, telling of the crucifixion and future reign of the Messiah King.

Jesus' agony on the cross was very real. The nails that pierced His hands hurt Him as much as they would hurt us if we were hanging there. But Jesus knew that his suffering was not a victory for Satan and the forces of evil, but part of God's plan. Jesus praised God *for* the suffering, because He knew it would bring the final victory over evil in the world.

"My God, my God, why have You forsaken me?" Jesus cried out, and the Psalm continues, "Why are You so far from helping me, and from the words of my groaning? ... But You are holy, O You Who dwell in ... the praises of Israel ... Our fathers trusted in You; they ... were confident — and You delivered them ... But I am ... the scorn of men , and despised by the people. Everyone who sees me mocks and sneers and shrugs. 'Is this the one who claims the Lord delights in him? We'll believe it when we see God rescue him!' ... I am surrounded by fearsome enemies, strong as the giant bulls from Bashan. They come at me with open jaws, like roaring lions attacking their prey. My strength has drained away like water, and all my bones are out of joint. My heart melts like wax; my strength has dried up like sun-baked clay; my tongues sticks to my mouth, for you have laid me in the dust of death. The enemy, this gang of evil men, circles me like a pack of dogs; they have pierced my hands and feet. I can count every bone in my body. See these men of evil gloat and stare; they divide my clothes among themselves by a toss of the dice. But be not far from me, O Lord; O my help, hasten to aid me! I will praise you to all my brothers; I will stand up before the congregation and testify of the wonderful things you have done. 'Praise the Lord, each one of you who fears him; I will say. 'Each of you must fear and reverence his name. Let all Israel sing his praises, for he has not despised my cries of deep despair; he has not turned and walked away. When I cried to him, he heard and came. Yes, I will stand and praise you before all people. I will publicly fulfill my vows in the presence of all who reverence your name.

"The poor shall eat and be satisfied; all who seek the Lord shall find him and shall praise his name. Their hearts shall rejoice with everlasting joy. The whole earth shall see it and return to the Lord; the people of every nation shall worship him. For the Lord is King and rules the nations. Both proud and humble together, all who are mortal — born to die — shall worship him. Posterity shall serve him; they shall tell of the Lord to the next generation. They shall come and shall declare His righteousness to a people yet to be born, that He has done it" (*Living Bible* and *Amplified Bible*).

The *Amplified Bible* adds to the last line, "It is finished!" the last words Jesus breathed before He gave up His spirit and died (John 19:30).

Jesus had often referred to the prophet Isaiah who foretold with amazing accuracy His life and death and future reign.

"But He was wounded and bruised for *our* sins. He was chastised that we might have peace; he was lashed — and we were healed! We are the ones who strayed away like sheep! We, who left God's paths to follow our own. Yet God laid on him the guilt and sins of every one of us! He was oppressed and he was afflicted, yet he never said a word. He was brought as a lamb to the slaughter; and as a sheep before her shearers is dumb, so he stood silent before the ones condemning him. From prison and trial they led him away to his death. But who among the people of that day realized it was their sins that he was dying for — that he was suffering their punishment? He was buried like a criminal in a rich man's grave; but he had done no wrong, and had never spoken an evil word.

"Yet it was the Lord's good plan to bruise him and fill him with grief. But when his soul has been made an offering for sin, then he shall have a multitude of children, many heirs. He shall live again and God's program shall prosper in his hands. And when he sees all that is accomplished by the anguish of his soul, he shall be satisfied; and because of what he has experienced, my righteous Servant shall make many to be counted righteous before God, for he shall bear all their sins. Therefore I will give him the honors of one who is mighty and great, because he has poured out his soul unto death. He was counted as a sinner, and he bore the sins of many, and he pled with God for sinners'' (Isa. 53:5-12).

Jesus knew that His crucifixion was not a thwarting of God's plan, but a fulfillment of it. The disciples, however, didn't understand. They saw the crucifixion of Jesus as an end to all their hopes and dreams for the future. They didn't remember Jesus' words when He had told them, ''You have sorrow now, but I will see you again and then you will rejoice and no one can rob you of that joy'' (John 16:22).

The disciples weren't looking forward to seeing Jesus again, and when they were told that He was no longer in the tomb, they thought His body had been stolen.

Later that day, two of Jesus' followers walked along the road from Jerusalem, to Emmaus. They were talking about Jesus' death when suddenly Jesus Himself came and walked beside them. But they didn't recognize Him.

He looked at their sad faces and said, ''What are you so concerned about?''

''Haven't you heard?'' one of them named Cleopas said. ''You must be the only person in Jerusalem who hasn't heard about the terrible things that happened there last week.''

Jesus listened as they poured out their sad tale to Him, about the wonderful Jesus of Nazareth who had done such great miracles that they were sure He was the Messiah who had come to rescue Israel, but the religious leaders had handed Him over to the Roman government and He had been crucified. The men spoke as if they had just witnessed the greatest tragedy the world had ever known. On top of it all, they said, the body of Jesus was missing from the tomb, and some women said they'd seen angels who told them that Jesus was alive. The men seemed certain that the last bit of news could only be a fairy tale.

''Then Jesus said to them, 'You are such foolish, foolish people! You find it so hard to believe all that the prophets wrote in the Scriptures. Wasn't it clearly predicted by the prophets that the Messiah would have to suffer all these things before entering his time of glory?'

''Then Jesus quoted them passage after passage from the

writings of the prophets, beginning with the book of Genesis and going right on through the Scriptures, explaining what the passages meant and what they said about himself" (Luke 24:25-27).

By this time they were coming near Emmaus, and since it was getting late, the two men asked the stranger to spend the night with them. They still hadn't recognized Him!

Jesus came home with them, and when "they sat down to eat, he asked God's blessing on the food and then took a small loaf of bread and broke it and was passing it over to them, when suddenly — it was as though their eyes were opened — they recognized him!" (Luke 24:30-31).

At last they believed. But for so long they had been able to see only the outward circumstances and had completely missed seeing God's perfect plan unfolding.

The disciples had seen their leader crucified, an apparent triumph of evil over good, and they had taken it as proof that God was not present with them. Yet, had they believed God's Word spoken through the prophets, they would have taken the same circumstances as evidence that God *was* with them and working out His plan.

We, too, are like disciples. When trials and sorrows come our way, our first reaction is, 'Oh God, why have you forsaken me?"

But Jesus said, 'Here on the earth you *will* have many trials and sorrows; but cheer up, for I have overcome the world" (John 16:33).

If we truly believed the words of Jesus, we'd see our circumstances as evidence of God's presence with us, and we'd praise and thank Him for them, instead of complaining and grumbling.

We shake our head at the world conditions and say, "Now *there* is plenty of evidence that God isn't doing much these days."

But Jesus told his followers to expect wars, earthquakes, famines, insurrections, epidemics, pollution, sexual revolution, and so on down the list — a perfect picture of the world we live in, and a promise that it would be getting worse.

Jesus said, 'Now when these things begin to take place, look up and raise your heads, because your redemption is drawing near!'' (Luke 21:28 RSV).

When things get worse in this world of ours, it is no evidence that God is absent or indifferent. Quite the contrary. All these signs are evidence that God is very near, that every part of His plan and purpose is being fulfilled, just as His Word has promised us.

Jesus told His disciples to rejoice with Him over His crucifixion. Had they been able to trust in His word, they could have experienced joy instead of grief. God's Word tells us to rejoice in our trials.

Peter wrote, "Trust [ing in Jesus] . . . even now you are happy with the inexpressible joy that comes from heaven itself" (I Pet. 1:8).

So what will you believe? Will you walk along your road as did the two men going toward Emmaus, saddened and preoccupied by the outward circumstances, convinced that God is far away? Or will you let your eyes be opened and be thankful?

Receive the bread, the Word, the life, the peace, the joy that Jesus is offering you. See that Jesus is with you, and that God is working in every circumstance of your life to meet your need.

The very thing you think is painful proof of God's absence from your life is in fact His living provision to draw you toward Himself — so that your joy may be full!

Look up and praise Him! He loves you, and He dwells in the praises of His people!

LET ALL THE JOYS OF THE GODLY WELL UP IN PRAISE TO THE LORD, for it is right to praise him!

Play joyous melodies of praise upon the lyre and on the harp!

Compose new songs of praise to him, accompanied skillfully on the harp; sing joyfully.

For all God's words are right, and everything he does is worthy of our trust.

He loves whatever is just and good; the earth is filled with his tender love.

He merely spoke, and the heavens were formed, and all the galaxies of stars.

He made the oceans, pouring them into his vast reservoirs.

Let everyone in all the world — men, women and children — fear the Lord and stand in awe of him.

For when he but spoke, the world began! It appeared at his command!

And with a breath he can scatter the plans of all the nations who oppose him, but His own plan stands forever. His intentions are the same for every generation.

Blessed is the nation whose God is the Lord, whose people he has chosen as his own.

The Lord gazes down upon mankind from heaven where he lives. He has made their hearts and closely watches everything they do.

The best-equipped army cannot save a king — for great strength is not enough to save anyone. A war horse is a poor risk for winning victories — it is strong but it cannot save.

But the eyes of the Lord are watching over those who fear him, who rely upon his steady love.

He will keep them from death even in time of famine!

We depend upon the Lord alone to save us. Only he can help us; he protects us like a shield.

No wonder we are happy in the Lord! For we are trusting him! We trust his holy name.

Yes, Lord, let your constant love surround us, for our hopes are in you alone.

—Psalm 33

You will also want to read these other best-sellers by Merlin Carothers:

PRISON TO PRAISE

Merlin Carothers' first book. This book has been printed in thirty-one languages and distributed in over sixty countries. Many people have reported transformed lives as a result of reading the powerful message found in this book.

ANSWERS TO PRAISE

The proof of the pudding! No sooner did the first two Praise Books come out than the phone calls and letters started pouring in. Praise works! Over-joyed Christians felt compelled to share the "signs and wonders following" with the author, adding their own testimonies to the rapidly-growing record. Miracle upon miracle, from all walks of life!

PRAISE WORKS

More letters selected from an assortment of thousands illustrate the secret of *freedom through praise!* Includes a letter from Frank Foglio — (author of *Hey, God!*) — who learned the power of praise when his daughter recovered miraculously after 7 long years in the "hopeless" ward of an institution for the mentally ill. Other letters are from a nurse, a nun, an attorney, a blind girl, a chaplain, an alcoholic and many others! Praise for brain surgery, praise for prison, praise for the Lord!

WALKING AND LEAPING

When Merlin Carothers lost a new car and trailer, along with his most-prized possessions, in a freak traffic accident — he praised God. But when he found himself singlehandedly overseeing the construction of a massive church building with only the enthusiastic but unskilled labor of his parishioners, and with the precarious backing of a bank balance that generally registered zero, he had to learn to "praise God in all things" all over again. "Fascinating and exciting. I thoroughly enjoyed it."

— New Life Magazine

BRINGING HEAVEN INTO HELL

Now Merlin Carothers goes beyond his earlier works to explore life-changing situations which others have experienced. The author shares these discoveries of God's forgiveness, a new freedom in Christ and the power of the Holy Spirit to shed light from heaven in the midst of a personal hell.

VICTORY ON PRAISE MOUNTAIN

When Merlin Carothers met with contention and dissension in his church, he learned to apply in his own life the principles he has taught to millions of others. This intensely personal account shows how genuine, spontaneous praise often leads into valleys that are direct paths to higher ground.

THE BIBLE ON PRAISE

This beautifully-printed, four-color, thirty-two page booklet features selected verses on praise from thirty-eight books of the Bible. These are Merlin's favorite verses and were personally selected by him. This booklet makes a lovely gift with a message that will bless the reader for years.

MORE POWER TO YOU

Worldwide demand for more information on power has resulted in *More Power To You* — written for persons in everyday places who need more power in their everyday lives. Though presented in simple easy-to-read language, the author has given us profound and useful insights into serious problems of modern life. This book is a beautiful key to unlock a vast storehouse of spiritual power.

WHAT'S ON YOUR MIND?

Imagine a motion-picture screen above your head. Now, visualize on that screen the thoughts that have come to your mind in recent weeks. Would you be ashamed for everyone you know to see your thoughts? If so, you urgently need to read and understand *What's on Your Mind?*

ALSO AVAILABLE ON CASSETTE:

Prison To Praise (set of 6 teaching tapes)
Power In Praise (set of 6 teaching tapes)

COMMENTS on Merlin Carothers' latest book, WHAT'S ON YOUR MIND?

THE WHITE HOUSE — Herb Ellingwood — *Legal Counsel to President Reagan: "What's on Your Mind?* is the best book I have read in years —for me and for the nation! Thanks for being receptive to God's message. Please send 100 copies. I believe this is what our governmental leaders need."

Two Months Later: "We are now using *What's on Your Mind?* in our weekly Bible study group."

ASTRONAUT — James Irwin — who walked on the moon: "Excellent! Courageous! Please send 30 copies."

PRESIDENT OF ASBURY THEOLOGICAL SEMINARY — David L. McKenna: "I have reviewed *What's on Your Mind?* Please send a copy for each of our forty faculty members."

EDITOR FOR CHOSEN BOOKS — David Manuel: "This will be the number one Christian book this year."

AUTHOR — Judson Cornwall: "It addresses a deep need. It is good!"

AD AGENCY VICE-PRESIDENT — Dick Meyers: "This is Merlin's best book."

PASTORS: "Every pastor in the world must read this book. I have read thousands of books, and this is the first time I have made such a statement."

"When I read *What's on Your Mind?* I felt as though God had a searchlight on my soul."

TEACHER: "The first book I have read that is pertinent and superb for teenagers and senior citizens."

LAYMEN: *"What's on Your Mind?* set me free from a burden I had carried over 25 years. Every Christian in the world must read this book."

"This is the most unusual book I have read during my 35 years as a Christian."

If this book has been a blessing to you, please let me
know. Each month I prepare Praise News in which I
share new things that I learn about praise. I will be
pleased to send this to you at no charge if you request it.

Write to:

Merlin R. Carothers
Box 2518
Escondido, CA 92025